# Peer Response in Second Language Writing Classrooms

**Michigan Series on Teaching Multilingual Writers**

**Series Editors**
**Diane Belcher (Ohio State University) and**
**Jun Liu (University of Arizona)**

*Available titles in the series*

*Peer Response in Second Language Writing Classrooms*
    Jun Liu & Jette G. Hansen

*Treatment of Error in Second Language Student Writing*
    Dana R. Ferris

# Peer Response in Second Language Writing Classrooms

## Jun Liu
University of Arizona

## Jette G. Hansen
University of Arizona

 Michigan Series on Teaching Multilingual Writers

*Ann Arbor*
THE UNIVERSITY OF MICHIGAN PRESS

Copyright © by the University of Michigan 2002
All rights reserved
Published in the United States of America by
The University of Michigan Press
Manufactured in the United States of America
♾ Printed on acid-free paper

2005   2004   2003   2002      4   3   2   1

*A CIP catalog record for this book is available from the British Library.*

**Library of Congress Cataloging-in-Publication Data**

Liu, Jun, 1959–
    Peer response in second language writing classrooms / Jun Liu,
Jette G. Hansen.
        p.     cm.
    Includes bibliographical references.
    ISBN 0-472-08808-4 (pbk. : alk. paper)
    1. Language and languages—Study and teaching.   2. Composition
(Language arts)   3. Rhetoric—Study and teaching.   4. Group work in
education.   I. Hansen, Jette G., 1967–   II. Title.
P53.27.L58      2002
418′.0071—dc21                                          2001007076

# Contents

Series Foreword by Diane Belcher    vii
List of Tables    ix
List of Peer Response Forms    x

**Introduction    1**
Theoretical Justifications    2
Pedagogical Considerations    7
The Structure of the Book    12

**1. Effects of Peer Response    14**
Motivational Effects: Perceptions of Peer Response    14
Short-Term Effects: The Effects of Peer Response
    on Revision    22
Long-Term Effects: The Effects of Peer Response on Language
    Development    27
Suggestions for Teachers    29

**2. Contexts of Peer Response: Types of Programs
   and Levels of Students    32**
Second Language versus Foreign Language Settings    32
Types of Students    44
Suggestions for Teachers    55

**3. Grouping Students in Peer Response    58**
Definition of a Group    58
Group Formation    60
Sustaining Group Work    67
Suggestions for Teachers    75

**4. Modes and Roles in Peer Response   80**

Modes of Peer Response   81

Roles in Peer Response   89

Suggestions for Teachers   97

**5. Foci of Peer Response   100**

Focus on Content   104

Focus on Rhetoric and Organization   110

Focus on Grammar and Style   114

Focus on a Combination of Features   117

Suggestions for Teachers   119

**6. Instructing Students in Peer Response   122**

The Rationale for Instruction   123

Instruction for Responding   125

The Modes of Instruction   140

The Timing of Peer Response   151

Instruction for Revision   151

Suggestions for Teachers   155

**7. Making Peer Response Effective   157**

Problems and Solutions   157

Final Checklist for Peer Response   164

References   169

Subject Index   177

Author Index   181

# Series Foreword

In the fields of language teaching and the teaching of writing there has been much discussion over the last two to three decades of the value of group work. The learner-centered methodology of the communicative language teaching approach and the privileging of peer collaboration by writing process advocates, both as a means of expanding the audience beyond the teacher and providing a supportive, facilitative environment, have helped make peer response activities commonplace in the second language (L2) writing classroom. Yet the research findings in this area, L2 peer responding, have not conclusively pointed to its usefulness; and a number of experienced L2 writing teachers, perhaps because of their own students' resistance to peer responding activities, have wondered aloud at conferences and other forums about the wisdom of adopting this particular process writing tool. For all these reasons—the pervasiveness of peer response in L2 writing classes as well as the continuing controversy over its appropriateness and uncertainty about its effectiveness for L2 writers—Jun Liu and Jette Hansen's volume on peer response is an extremely welcome addition to the Michigan Series on Teaching Multilingual Writers, a series committed to addressing key topics in the teaching of L2 writing.

Readers of this volume will no doubt be struck by how well acquainted Liu and Hansen are with the research and how straightforwardly they communicate its many findings. Obvious too will be the fact that both have utilized peer response in their own writing classes, are aware of the challenges it poses, and have developed successful problem-solving strategies. Liu and Hansen's dual perspective as both scholars and practitioners clearly has enabled them to produce a volume that is not only informed by a careful, comprehensive review of research but also highly accessible and applicable for teachers and teacher-trainees. Classroom practitioners will likely be especially pleased to see the wealth of ancillary materials provided in this volume, including guiding questions for a wide variety of writing tasks. Perhaps more noteworthy, though, is the sensitivity that the authors demonstrate and encourage to the impact of various educational and cultural backgrounds on reaction to peer work. Because of their own experiences as students and as teachers, the authors are very conscious of the need for thoughtful, well-planned preparation of students for collaborative work and the benefits of a sensitive, supportive teacher throughout the peer responding process.

It is probably quite safe to say that no prior work has attempted to offer so extensive and intensive a look at the issues and strategies of peer response in linguistically diverse settings. Experienced and inexperienced writing teachers alike should find much of value here: a single volume that provides access to the most relevant research on peer response, applies it to the L2 writing context, and hence can inform decisions on when, how, and why to use (or not to use) peer responding activities with multilingual writers.

Diane Belcher, Ohio State University

# Tables

Table 1.   Benefits and Constraints in Using Peer
Response   8

Table 2.   Levels of Students' Positive Experiences
with Peer Response   18

Table 3.   Teacher and Student Scenarios across Foreign
and Second Language Contexts 35

Table 4.   Skill-Area Problems and Solutions in Peer
Response   41

Table 5.   Guiding Questions for Peer Response with
Younger Writers   50

Table 6.   Benefits and Constraints of Different Peer
Response Modes   88

Table 7.   Responsibilities of Peer Response Facilitator   94

Table 8.   Probing Questions for Focusing on Content   109

Table 9.   Probing Questions for Focusing on Rhetoric
and Organization   113

Table 10.  Time Line for a Combination of Foci   119

Table 11.  Guidelines for Preparing Students for Peer
Response   129

Table 12.  Organizing a Portfolio of Students' Sample
Drafts/Peer Responses   132

Table 13.  Question and Comment Types in Peer
Response   138

Table 14.  Useful Sentences for Peer Response
Activities   141

Table 15.  Revision Feedback Sheet   153

# Peer Response Forms

Example 1. Peer Response Sheet for a "Process" Paragraph (beginning or lower-intermediate students)   134

Example 2. Peer Response Sheet for a "Problem/Solution" Essay (intermediate or upper-intermediate students)   135

Example 3. Peer Response Sheet for a "Definition" Task (intermediate or upper-intermediate students)   136

Example 4. Peer Response Sheet for a "Critical Review" Task (advanced students)   137

Example 5. Peer Response Sheet for a "Problem/Solution" Task (lower-intermediate students)   143

Example 6. Peer Response Sheet for a "Problem/Solution" Task (upper-intermediate students)   144

Example 7. Peer Response Sheet for a "Problem/Solution" Task (advanced students)   144

Example 8. Peer Response Sheet for a "Problem/Solution" Task (mixed-level students)   145

Example 9. Flexible Peer Response Sheet for a "Problem/Solution" Task (all levels)   148

# Introduction

For many years, the unique benefits language learners can offer to each other were ignored in L2 writing classrooms. Such a failure to recognize the contributions that L2 learners can make to each other has given way to an active effort to tap the potential of learners as teachers and tutors in L2 writing processes. This has given rise to *peer response* as part of the process approach to teaching L2 writing. Peer response activities, in which students work together to provide feedback on one another's writing in both written and oral formats through active engagement with each other's progress over multiple drafts, have become a common feature of L2 writing instruction. As such, there is a need to discuss peer response in L2 writing in greater depth so that the research findings in this area can be closely examined in contextualized L2 teaching scenarios within a unified theoretical framework. This book is offered to fill this void.

In this book, "peer response" is used as an umbrella term to designate what is normally referred to as "peer feedback," "peer review," or "peer editing" in teaching L2 writing. Although the term is probably easily understood, it might be helpful to define it clearly from the outset. *Peer response is the use of learners as sources of information and interactants for each other in such a way that learners assume roles and responsibilities normally taken on by a formally trained teacher, tutor, or editor in commenting on and critiquing each other's drafts in both written and oral formats in the process of writing.* Due to the collaborative nature and to the employment of both written and oral formats in this activity, the more general term "peer response" is used. In this introduction, we discuss the theoretical stances of peer response, the pedagogical implications of peer response, and the structure of this book.

The intended audience of this book is threefold. The first readership includes those teachers who used or are using peer response activities in their L2 writing classrooms. For members of this group, the book will serve as a stimulus to help them reflect on their own practices in using peer response as a regular classroom activity. The second readership includes those who are or who will be teaching L2 writing courses yet have never incorporated or are not yet planning to use peer response activities in their L2 writing classrooms. For members of this group, the book will serve as a guide to show them what can be done and how. The third readership includes those who are skeptical about peer response and those who have used peer response but found their practice ineffective in one way or another. For members of this group, the book provides numerous examples and analyses to show why the expected results are sometimes not achieved in conducting peer response activities, what the potential problems are with peer response activities, and how to resolve them.

## Theoretical Justifications

Why should peer response activities be used in teaching L2 writing? There are four theoretical stances, which in fact complement and to some extent overlap each other, that support the use of peer response activities in the writing classroom from both cognitive and psycholinguistic perspectives: *process writing theory, collaborative learning theory, Vygotsky's Zone of Proximal Development,* and *interaction and second language acquisition* (SLA). Research based on these theoretical stances has provided substantial evidence that peer response activities in fact help second language learners develop not only their L2 writing abilities but also their overall L2 language abilities through the negotiation of meaning that typically takes place during peer response.

## Process Writing Theory

The process approach to writing emerged in the late 1960s and early 1970s in L1 writing (e.g., Elbow 1973; Emig 1971; Moffett 1968) as a response to the traditional *product* views of writing that focused on form over meaning and the finished text rather than on the *process* in which writing took place. As such, the process approach to writing, which heavily influenced L2 writing theory and practice, focused on the process of writing, viewing writing not as a product-oriented activity but rather one that is dynamic, nonlinear, and recursive. In pedagogical practice, students are encouraged to engage in multiple drafting, and writing is viewed as occurring in stages that may differ to some extent among different writers. Typically, textbooks and courses following the process approach to writing encourage writers to engage in *brainstorming* activities, *outlining, drafting* (focusing on meaning), *rewriting* (focusing on organization and meaning), and *editing* (focusing on style and grammar).

Within this approach to writing, peer response has been viewed as an important component of L2 writing instruction (Kroll 1991; Leki 1990; Mangelsdorf 1989; Mangelsdorf and Schlumberger 1992; Mittan 1989; Zamel 1985). Peer response supports process writing with a focus on drafting and revision and enables students to get multiple feedback (e.g., from teacher, peer, and self) across various drafts. Additionally, it builds audience awareness; helps make reading-writing connections; and builds content, linguistic, and rhetorical schemata through multiple exposures to a text.

## Collaborative Learning Theory

Another theoretical framework that promotes the use of collaborative group work is collaborative learning theory. A central tenet in collaborative learning theories is that learning, as well as knowledge itself, is socially constructed. Bruffee (1984), a leading proponent of collaborative writing, defines collaborative learning as the type of learning that takes place through communication with peers and states that there are certain kinds of knowledge that are best acquired in this manner. Collaborative learning theories have had a major impact on L1 writing instruction and more recently have begun to have an impact on both theoretical and pedagogical aspects of L2 writing.

Research in L1 writing has found numerous benefits of employing collaborative learning techniques in the classroom. Studies have found that in writing groups, students negotiate meaning as they help each other revise their papers (Gere 1987) and that learning in writing groups is reciprocal and improves students' work (Bruffee 1984). As Bruffee (1984, 644) states, while students individually may not have all the knowledge or resources available to successfully complete a task, "pooling the resources that a group of peers brings with them to the task" may enable the group to complete a task that individuals may not be able to complete on their own.

L2 writing group researchers have also found that there are a number of linguistic gains of collaborative writing and revising. For example, researchers have found that collaborative writing groups can lead to decision making, "allow[ing] learners to compare notes on what they have learned and how to use it effectively" and providing learners with "increased opportunities to review and apply their growing knowledge of second language (L2) writing through dialogue and interaction with their peers in the writing group" (Hirvela 1999, 8). This is not surprising and in fact echoes the findings of research on interaction and SLA, as outlined later in this chapter, since peer response activities are one kind of collaborative group work that may lead to greater opportunities for students to negotiate meaning as they work with peers in improving a written text.

### Vygotsky's Zone of Proximal Development

A third theoretical stance that supports the use of peer response in the writing classroom is based on Vygotsky's (1978) belief that cognitive development is a result of social interaction in which an individual learns to extend her or his current competence through the guidance of a more experienced individual. Simply stated, "Social interaction is a mechanism for individual development, since, in the presence of a more capable participant, the novice is drawn into, and operates within, the space of the expert's strategic processes for problem solving" (Donato 1994, 37). The space between the person's actual level of development (i.e., what can be done independently) and the potential level of development (i.e., what can be done with the help of someone else) is called the Zone of Proximal Development (ZPD). Higher cognitive processes are hypothesized to emerge as a result of interaction, resulting in the individual's independent completion of the task, with the language use within the interaction serving as the "critical device for mediating cognitive development" (DiCamilla and Anton 1997, 614). While Vygotsky originally developed the notion of the ZPD to account for child development and considered the novice as a child and the more experienced individual as a guiding adult, his work has since been further developed by L1 researchers such as Wood, Bruner, and Ross (1976), who employ the term "scaffolding" to describe the supportive conditions that occur within the ZPD. Vygotsky's theoretical framework has been employed by L2 researchers such as Donato (1994) and Lantolf and Appel (1994) to investigate interaction in group work and by L2 writing researchers (Guerrero and Villamil 1994; DiCamilla and Anton 1997; Villamil and Guerrero 1996, 1998) to examine how peer response activities during group work in the second language writing classroom influences language learning.

Results of the research (e.g., Guerrero and Villamil 1994; DiCamilla and Anton 1997; Donato 1994; Villamil and Guerrero 1996) indicate that collective scaffolding occurs in group work, wherein "the speakers are at the same time individually novices and collectively experts, sources of new orientations for each other, and guides through this complex linguistic problem solving" (Donato 1994, 46). Furthermore, long-term language development was found as a result of this collective scaffolding (Donato 1994). In addition, peer response activities "foster a myriad of communicative behaviors" that benefit all members of a group (Villamil and Guerrero 1996, 69).

## Interaction and Second Language Acquisition

Over the past 20 years, researchers (e.g., Doughty and Pica 1986; Long 1985; Long et al. 1976; Long and Porter 1985; Pica and Doughty 1985; Pica et al. 1989; Porter 1983, 1986; Varonis and Gass 1983) have begun recognizing that there are a number of psycholinguistic rationales for using group work. The findings of the research on interaction and second language acquisition provide clear evidence that engaging learners in group activities that require students to negotiate meaning, such as peer response activities, enables learners to gain additional practice in the target language. Group work increases opportunities for students to engage in the negotiation of meaning, and the increased opportunities to negotiate meaning may lead to increased comprehension, which leads to faster and better acquisition. Furthermore, group work pushes learners to produce comprehensible output, which some researchers (e.g., Swain 1985) believe is necessary in order for second language acquisition to take place. Long and Porter (1985, 221–22) list a number of other psycholinguistic reasons for group work: (1) increased quantity of practice, especially in two-way communication tasks; (2) increased range of language functions utilized; (3) similar levels of accuracy in student production as in teacher-led activities; (4) increased error correction in group work (students almost never miscorrect); and (5) increased negotiation of meaning.

## Summary

Research based on process writing, collaborative learning theory, Vygotsky's Zone of Proximal Development, and interaction and second language acquisition indicates that there is ample evidence that language learners need to be engaged in interactive activities that create opportunities for them to negotiate meaning and to learn from and implicitly teach peers in order to promote second language learning, including L2 writing development. Peer response activities, which involve problem-solving tasks focused on improving the quality of a written draft, provide learners with the opportunities necessary to test their knowledge, learn from their peers, and negotiate meaning—all of which have been shown to be important in the development of second language skills.

## Pedagogical Considerations

Now that peer response activities have been supported by process writing theory, collaborative learning theory, Vygotsky's ZPD, and interaction and second language acquisition, what are some of the pedagogical benefits of peer response? Over the past decade, many L2 writing instructors have been trying to incorporate peer response activities in their ESL writing classes and have been convinced of their beneficial effects on motivation, attitude, and even on writing quality (e.g., Allaei and Connor 1990; Mittan 1989). But they have also experienced constraints in using peer response in their L2 writing classrooms. The benefits and the constraints of peer review can be summarized in four major categories—namely, cognitive, social, linguistic, and practical, as shown in table 1.

### Benefits of Peer Response Activities

*Cognitively* speaking, peer response activities in teaching L2 writing can force L2 students to exercise their thinking as opposed to passively receiving information from the teacher (Mittan 1989). Students engaged in the peer response process can take an active role in their learning, and they can "reconceptualize their ideas in light of their peers' reactions" (Mendonça and Johnson 1994, 746). In peer response, students can engage in unrehearsed, low-risk, exploratory talk that is less feasible in whole-class and teacher-student interactions (Ferris and Hedgcock 1998). Responding to peers' writing, for instance, builds the critical skills needed to analyze and revise one's own writing (Leki 1990). Moreover, the suggestions and explanations offered during the peer response activities allow students to show what they know about writing and to use that information in their revisions (Mendonça and Johnson 1994). In addition, peer response activities allow students to develop audience awareness, and the fact that writers revise their essays based on their peers' comments suggests that peer response activities "develop in students the crucial ability of reviewing their writing with the eyes of another" (Zamel 1982, 206) and allow them to modify their written texts to meet the

**TABLE 1.    Benefits and Constraints in Using Peer Response**

|  | Cognitive | Social | Linguistic | Practical |
|---|---|---|---|---|
| Benefits | 1. Exercise thinking<br>2. Take active role in learning<br>3. Engage in exploratory talk<br>4. Build critical skills<br>5. Demonstrate and reinforce knowledge<br>6. Build audience awareness | 1. Enhance communicative power<br>2. Receive authentic feedback<br>3. Gain confidence and reduce apprehension<br>4. Establish collegial ties and friendship<br>5. Influence learners' affective state | 1. Enhance metalinguistic knowledge<br>2. Explore linguistic knowledge<br>3. Gain additional language skill practice<br>4. Enhance participation and improve discourse<br>5. Find right words to express ideas | 1. Applicable across student proficiency levels<br>2. Flexible across different stages in the writing process<br>3. Time-efficient in some cases<br>4. Reinforces process writing |
| Constraints | 1. Uncertainty concerning peers' comments<br>2. Lack of learner investment | 1. Discomfort and uneasiness<br>2. Lack of security in negotiating meaning<br>3. Commentary may be overly critical | 1. Too much focus on surface structure<br>2. Lack of L2 formal schemata<br>3. Difficulty in understanding foreign accent | 1. Time constraints<br>2. Counter-productive feedback<br>3. Lack of student preparation |

needs of their audience. In peer response activities, students are talking about what they have learned or what they are learning. Instead of working independently on their own writing, students are continually talking about their writing, reinforcing knowledge they have already acquired but feel uncertain about, and filling in gaps in their understanding of what they have learned (Hirvela 1999). Writing groups also help writers develop a sense of audience and compel them to revise as they negotiate meaning with their readers (Gere 1987).

Peer response activities also have many *social* benefits. For instance, they enhance students' communicative power by encouraging students to express and negotiate their ideas (Mendonça and Johnson 1994). In the process of responding to their peers, students constantly receive "reactions, questions, and responses from authentic readers" (Mittan 1989, 209), so that they gain a clearer understanding of what has been done well and what remains unclear. Peer response activities help students gain confidence and reduce apprehension by allowing them to see peers' strengths and weaknesses in writing (Leki 1990). In peer response, students experience excellent opportunities to establish collegial ties with other students who share the same concerns and backgrounds as they do. The dynamics involved in peer response activities may offer comfortable and secure learning situations to students who otherwise may feel isolated and misunderstood. They also may open up new avenues for friendship through students' collaboration (Hirvela 1999).

In terms of *linguistic* benefits, the collaborative setting in which peer response activities take place allows students to review the metalanguage of reading and writing supplied in a course as they use technical terminology in their discussions (Gere 1987). Through collaborative group production, students experience valuable opportunities to improve their ability to read and write because the ongoing community orientation of this approach enables them to draw on the strengths and resources of their peers while sorting through their own growing knowledge of L2 writing (Hirvela 1999).

Students are able to practice the target language in authentic and meaningful communicative contexts as they interact with each other while completing collaborative tasks such as peer response activities. They also have a chance to explore the target language as they respond to their peers' drafts and discuss such issues as appropriate word choice and grammatical structures. An added benefit of peer response activities for many L2 contexts (e.g., with preadmission or postadmission students, immigrants, or adult education students) is that students gain additional practice with other language skills, thereby enhancing their overall English language proficiency. In fact, group work increases individual students' participation in terms of conversational turns (Pica and Doughty 1985), and it provides opportunities for learners to go beyond sentence-level discourse, practice turn-taking strategies appropriate for the target language, engage in unplanned speech, and receive exposure to sociolinguistic contexts otherwise unavailable to them. Peer interactions can help L2 students communicate their ideas and enhance the development of L2 learning in general (Mangelsdorf 1989). In addition, audience feedback is important in SLA as students must test out and revise their hypotheses about the second language in meaningful contexts. In sum, peer response activities give students more ways to discover and explore ideas, to find the right words to express their ideas, and to negotiate with their audience about these ideas.

On a *practical* level, peer response activities are flexible, as they can take place at various stages of the writing process (prewriting/discovery/invention, between-draft revision, and editing) (Connor and Asenavage 1994), and they fit well with the increased emphasis on process in composition teaching. Moreover, peer response activities can reduce the writing teacher's workload and can impart to the teacher important information about individual students' reading and writing abilities and their understanding of what constitutes good writing (Mittan 1989). Furthermore, peer response activities with the instructor participating by assuming the role of a peer can be highly time-efficient (Liu 1998).

### Constraints of Peer Response Activities

There are four legitimate and recurring reservations concerning the use of peer response activities in the teaching of L2 composition: *uncertainty concerning peers' comments, lack of learner investment, superficial comments due to time constraints,* and *inappropriate interactions in commenting on peers' drafts* (Liu 1998). In peer response activities, students often feel uncertain as to whether their peers' comments are accurate. Their insecurity can lead to a lack of enthusiasm toward this activity. Meanwhile, some students may come to peer response sessions underprepared, thus "seriously hindering the mutual exchange among peers and demonstrating a lack of respect for others" (Liu 1998, 237).

It is commonly understood that peer response activities suffer from several drawbacks. Students sometimes focus too heavily on "surface concerns" (Leki 1990, 9), or editing, neglecting larger revising issues. They provide vague and unhelpful comments; are hostile, sarcastic, overly critical, or unkind in their criticisms of their classmates' writing; feel uncertain about the validity of their classmates' responses; struggle with their own listening comprehension skills because of foreign accents; and have a lack of a formal L2 (rhetorical) schemata, which may lead to inappropriate expectations about the content and structure of peers' texts, resulting in counterproductive feedback that leads writers further away from academic expectations. In addition, the interactions of the group are at times unpleasant, with students being overly critical of each other's writings (Nelson and Murphy 1992). In fact, the nature of responding to peers' drafts sometimes generates a sense of discomfort and uneasiness among the participants. Generally speaking, the students could become rather defensive when their work is criticized, especially by their peers (Amores 1997).

### Summary

Peer response activities in teaching L2 writing have revealed both strengths and weaknesses in four major areas. Cognitively speaking, peer response activities help students take charge of their own learning, build critical thinking skills, and consolidate their own knowledge of writing, although sometimes peer comments could be questionable and thus difficult to incorporate in revision. In terms of the social effects, peer response activities can enhance students' communication, build their social skills, and provide them with a supportive social network, although they sometimes can also be anxiety provoking and lead to communication breakdown. Linguistically, peer response activities are considered good opportunities for students to build their own linguistic knowledge, enhance participation, and improve both oral and written discourse, although students tend to overemphasize local structural and/or grammatical comments. From a pedagogical perspective, peer response activities can be done across students' proficiency levels and at different stages of writing, although time-efficiency is of great concern.

## The Structure of the Book

This book conforms to the major characteristics of the Teaching Multilingual Writers series—comprehensibility, illustrativeness, and research-based data—in dealing with the topical issue—peer response—from the three perspectives of teachers, learners, and researchers. All the chapters in the book are centered around the questions teachers of multilingual writers usually encounter in their daily classroom practice. Including an overview of the literature on peer response in L2 writing over the past two decades, the chapters focus on salient issues, such as the effects of peer response (chap. 1), contexts of peer response (chap. 2), grouping students in peer response (chap. 3), modes and roles in peer response (chap. 4), foci of peer response (chap. 5), instructing students in peer response (chap. 6), and making peer response effective (chap. 7).

Within the discussion of each issue, the questions are addressed through various examples of learners at different proficiency levels (beginning, intermediate, and advanced) in a variety of programs (preadmission and postadmission) and in several teaching contexts (ESL and EFL). Research findings, both positive and negative, are used to elucidate our discussion rather than as a priority in guiding the discussion. In each chapter, apart from the topical discussion prompted by teacher-initiated questions, we offer our comments, explanations, and suggestions for teachers and students, which we believe will be beneficial in assisting teachers to use peer response activities in their classrooms effectively and efficiently. For example, chapter 1 discusses three areas in which the effects of peer response seem to be obvious—namely, students' perceptions, revisions, and long-term learning. In our discussion of these areas, several issues are examined.

- In terms of students' perceptions, what perceptions do students generally hold toward peer response? What are students' preconceptualizations and postconceptualizations of peer response? What are the salient factors that determine students' perceptions of peer response?
- In terms of the effects of peer response activities on students' revisions, can students detect problems in their peers' texts and offer suggestions on how to correct them? What kinds of errors do students usually detect (surface, rhetorical, content)? Whose feedback do students adopt in revision, feedback from peer or self or teacher? Does peer response lead to quality revisions?
- Regarding the long-term effects on students' language learning, are the benefits of peer response short term? Or does it have long-term effects on students' overall language development?

This book concludes with chapter 7, which presents problems and solutions in peer response and a final checklist for teachers to use before engaging in peer response activities.

# Chapter 1

## Effects of Peer Response

What concerns both L2 writing teachers and students most about peer response activities is their effectiveness. This brings up a number of questions. What constitutes effective peer response in ESL/EFL composition classrooms? Are students motivated to engage in peer response activities? How do their perceptions toward peer response evolve or change as a result of their peer response experiences? What effects do peer response activities have on students' revisions? Are the effects temporary—in other words, product-oriented, in terms of yielding only revisions in the writer's next draft— or can long-lasting effects be shown on a student's writing development in the second language? Each of these questions will be addressed as we examine the effects of peer response.

### Motivational Effects: Perceptions of Peer Response

One primary concern of teachers using peer response activities in their L2 writing classrooms is whether their students will be engaged in the activities and find peer response activities meaningful and valuable in their learning processes. As far as students are concerned, their perceptions toward peer response in L2 writing could be either negative, positive, or a combination of both, as a result of their prior experience with peer response or of their inexperience with peer response. While their positive experiences with peer response can lead to higher levels of engagement and productivity, their negative experiences or lack of interest in peer response can decrease their level of engagement and minimize their productivity. The questions we need to ask are:

- What do ESL/EFL students think about peer response activities in their composition classes?
- How do the ways they receive their peer feedback affect their perceptions toward peer response activities?
- When and how do we ask students for their perceptions toward peer response activities?
- What are some possible factors that affect ESL/EFL students' perceptions of peer response activities in their writing courses?

## What do ESL/EFL students think about peer response activities in their composition classes?

The fact that ESL/EFL students at all levels have mixed feelings about the effects of peer response activities is not surprising. Their preferences largely depend on their experiences with peer response, in terms of group dynamics and task variation, and on the quality of comments they receive from their peers. In general, L2 writing students concur that peer response activities help them understand their own drafts better through critiquing others' papers and thus help them construct and revise their own drafts. As one study indicated (Mangelsdorf 1992), despite the fact that some college ESL students in L2 composition classes were unhappy with their peers' advice and doubted the ability of some peers to critique their papers, many students were positive about their peer response experiences, believing that peer response activities helped them revise the content of their drafts. Some undergraduate ESL students felt that both reading peers' papers and receiving feedback from peers were helpful, although a few students were troubled by the tone and quality of the peer feedback (Leki 1990). Students in low-level ESL classes at a community college also found peer response activities beneficial, believing that peer response activities helped them formulate topic sentences more clearly; add details to their paragraphs; discover their own most frequent errors; and learn new vocabulary, organizational patterns, and grammatical structures from each other (Hansen and Liu 2000). At the graduate level, some students viewed peer response activities as beneficial because (1) reading their own drafts to peers helped them see their papers more clearly and (2) reading others' papers helped them compare their writing with others and learn new ideas (Mendonça and Johnson 1994). Commonly cited concerns regarding peer response activities are mistrust of peers' feedback and fear of being ridiculed by one's peers due to one's limited English proficiency (Nelson and Carson 1998).

### How do the ways students receive peer feedback affect their perceptions toward peer response activities?

It should be pointed out that students' perceptions of peer response activities are also affected by whether and when they receive their teacher's feedback or comments on their drafts. When students receive peer feedback at the same time as they receive their teacher's feedback, they tend to attend to the teacher's comments more carefully than their peers' comments for the obvious reason that it is the teacher who gives the grade. In comparing the preference for teacher feedback, peer feedback, or self-feedback, students prefer teacher feedback, then peer feedback, and finally self-feedback (Nelson and Carson 1998; Zhang 1995). However, the issue is not *whether* teacher feedback should be given while students receive peer feedback. Rather, it is *when* the teacher's feedback should be given so that peer feedback will still be considered as a necessary and important channel of feedback that students can benefit from. It is understood that whenever there is a conflict between teacher feedback and peer feedback, the students are likely to incorporate teacher feedback, and by their doing so, the role of peer feedback is diminished. Students tend to have negative attitudes toward such peer feedback. It is impractical for teachers to refrain from giving feedback, but it is important to manage the timing of teacher feedback so as to maximize the effects of peer feedback (see chap. 4 for a detailed account of the role of the teacher in peer response activities).

### When and how do we ask students for their perceptions toward peer response activities?

Students' perceptions toward peer response could differ dramatically depending on when and how they are asked about peer response. If students have a limited amount of exposure to peer response, their perceptions could be more superficial. In addition, students' perceptions of peer response collected through one questionnaire or interview do not help us understand the context in which their perceptions of peer response are formed and the process through which they construct their perceptions. Perceptions of L2 students toward peer response will be less meaningful if we do not have a frame of reference to help us assess to what extent our students have formed or changed their perceptions toward peer response over a period of time and how their prior experiences, or lack of experience, with peer response are shaped by their new experiences.

Liu (1997) conducted a comparative study of ESL students' pre- and postconceptualizations of peer response in a postadmission university ESL composition program in the United States. By comparing 14 students' preconceptualizations with their postconceptualizations over three consecutive peer response activities across three major writing assignments during a 10-week quarter, Liu found that positive experiences with peer response emerged at several levels. The students thought not merely that they could benefit from peer response by discovering problems in their drafts (textual level) but that they could also expand their knowledge and develop their thinking (cognitive level) and communicate and make friends with peers (communicative level). The students' perceptions of peer response at these three levels are illustrated in the quotes from their reflections in table 2.

**TABLE 2.   Levels of Students' Positive Experiences with Peer Response**

| | |
|---|---|
| Textual Level | . . . is **significantly useful** in checking and improving |
| | . . . **helps** me to make improvement on the following drafts |
| | . . . **was able to recognize my mistakes clearly** after peer reviewing |
| | . . . **usually find the weaknesses of my papers** based on their comments |
| | . . . **can clarify our paper** if I don't understand clearly about it in group review |
| Cognitive Level | . . . is **helpful** in developing students' knowledge about writing |
| | . . . **helped** me improve my critical thinking |
| | . . . **can help** the group members present their opinions and train them to think independently |
| | . . . **helped** me plan writing strategies appropriate to the assignment. |
| | . . . **can know my problems** and other students' opinions by peer review |
| | . . . would **make me be aware** of what I need to add or what I should delete in my writings |
| | . . . **would organize my idea more explicitly** with readers' responses |
| | . . . **find peer response helpful** in my planning, writing, and enjoying the classroom climate and graduate school experience |
| | . . . **can get much information** in peer response |
| Communicative Level | . . . **provides** an opportunity for me to listen to others' views on my work |
| | . . . **provides** good opportunities for us to speak and express our ideas |
| | . . . **gave** me an opportunity to interact with other students in the group |
| | . . . **might point out some points** that I could not notice in my writings |
| | . . . **can learn some different writing skills and ideas** from other members' writings |
| | . . . **can get objective opinions** from non-specialists |
| | . . . **can learn and revise our papers** based on the critiques, analysis, and recommendations from the group members |

While the students' experiences with peer response activities were positive overall, they also expressed negative feelings about it. One concern was the cross-disciplinary gap in understanding and critiquing peers' papers (e.g., response to field-specific topics by a general audience), and the other was uncertainty in trusting and accepting peers' comments psychologically and linguistically. As is discussed in chapter 3, having students from different disciplines read each other's papers has both advantages and disadvantages. An obvious benefit is that the paper has to be written very clearly in order to be understood, and thus the author has to keep the general audience in mind when writing. The main drawback of having people from other disciplines critique the paper is the restriction in readers' being able to fully understand the content and the field-specific jargon. In sum, students from the same discipline can give ideas to the writer, but students from different disciplines can point out portions of the text that are unclear (Mendonça and Johnson 1994).

### What are some possible factors that affect ESL/EFL students' perceptions of peer response activities in their writing courses?

Admittedly, students' perceptions of peer response can be affected by multiple factors, such as the linguistic and sociocultural backgrounds of the students, the proficiency levels of the students, the tasks, the genre, and the format/mode of reviewing.

In peer response, the group members' cultural backgrounds are salient with regard to how these activities are actualized and what consequences they will result in. In many ESL writing classes, teachers encounter students from various linguistic and sociocultural backgrounds. Due to such diversity, these students will sometimes approach peer response tasks differently, and they will also influence one another in the process of peer response. Although we cannot generalize about student behavior in making or receiving peers' comments, students from certain cultural backgrounds are likely to have preferences regarding level of participation, in terms of giving or receiving peers' comments. For example, in a study investigating Chinese- and Spanish-speaking students' perceptions of their interactions in peer response groups in an

ESL composition class, it was found that both the Chinese-
and the Spanish-speaking students preferred negative comments that identified problems in their drafts. However, although these students agreed on the criterion of change as a
mark of effectiveness, the Chinese students depended more
than the Spanish students on group consensus in their peer
groups (Nelson and Carson 1998). In another study of perceptions of peer response activities among graduate ESL students in a postadmission program, it was found that a Chinese
student's perception of peer response changed from negative
to more positive as a result of thorough preparation to meet
the challenge of another Chinese peer who raised a lot of questions on the paper being reviewed (Liu 1998). Therefore, we
should be careful in examining the perceptual differences regarding peer response activities of students from diverse cultural backgrounds.

Sometimes students' perceived level of language ability appears to contribute significantly to their receptivity of the
peer-editing process (Amores 1997). It is reasonable to assume
that when students feel they are somewhat better than their
peers, they are likely to participate more in the peer response
activities and in offering their comments on their peers' drafts
but might be less enthusiastic in receiving their peers' comments on their own drafts. This leads to the issue of the role
each student plays in the peer group and the perceived status
of the differential role played by each participant in a given
group. To make peer response activities work, maintaining
the equality of student roles is very important (see chap. 3 for
a detailed discussion of grouping in peer response).

In addition, students' perceptions of peer response are
largely related to the tasks that are required in peer response
activities. For instance, students might be asked to find the
strengths and weaknesses of their peers' drafts or they might
be requested to find the theme, depending on what type of paper they are writing. These peer response tasks, which are
usually specified in peer response sheets, clearly indicate the
focus of the students' response. Therefore, clear adherence to

these tasks will affect students' perceptions of the effectiveness of the responses they receive.

Closely related to the tasks, the genre or type of paper is also important in forming students' perceptions of peer response. For instance, in responding to narrative essays, students' comments might have a different focus than if they are responding to argumentative essays. If the focus of comments is skewed (e.g., if a student is expecting comments on the plot of the story and all she receives are grammatical comments), the author of the draft might feel disappointed and thus develop negative feelings about peer response.

Another factor that could contribute to student perceptions of peer response is the format/mode of peer response. For instance, while some students may feel more comfortable receiving peer feedback through E-mail or in writing, others might prefer meeting the writer face-to-face in order to clarify not only what was written but also why it was written in a particular way. Some students might feel that they can respond to a draft more objectively if the author's name is kept confidential, while some might feel that it is more helpful if they know whose paper they are responding to. These factors all contribute to the perceptions students hold of peer response activities.

In summary, there is much evidence that peer response activities are generally welcomed by students and that their perceptions of such activities are positive overall because of the benefits they receive: multiple perspectives on their writing, input on clarifying ideas, learning how to keep audience in mind while writing, and the raising of their consciousness toward their own writing. However, peer comments are less effective if the teacher's comments are offered concurrently. Therefore, caution should be used and teacher comments timed in order to maximize the effects of peer response activities. There are several other factors we need to consider, such as the task required, the genre of the paper under consideration, and the format/mode of peer response, in assessing students' perceptions of peer response activities in L2 writing classes.

## Short-Term Effects: The Effects of Peer Response on Revision

Aside from concerns about whether students will be engaged by and therefore motivated to complete peer response activities, many teachers also express concerns about whether peer-revision activities in fact help students write better papers. Teachers are often concerned about whether students have the linguistic, content-based, and rhetorical knowledge to enable them to give their peers constructive feedback on their drafts and whether the writers of the drafts will in turn modify their texts based on their peers' suggestions. Integral to the success of both of these facets of peer response is adequate instruction in how to properly respond to peers' writing, along with the teacher's availability to answer any linguistic or rhetorical questions that may arise as students negotiate the meaning of a text (see chap. 6). Our discussion here will focus on a number of common questions teachers and students have regarding the effects of peer response on revision.

### Can students detect problems in their peers' texts and offer suggestions on how to correct them?

A main concern of both teachers and students is whether students are in fact able to detect problems in their peers' texts and offer suggestions for correcting them. While a number of researchers have concluded that this is a problematic task for many L2 writers (e.g., Leki 1990; Nelson and Murphy 1992, 1993), other researchers have found that students, especially those who have been trained in peer response, are quite capable of making useful suggestions about their peers' drafts (e.g., Berg 1999; Hansen 2001; Hansen and Liu 2000; Hedgcock and Lefkowitz 1992; Paulus 1999; Stanley 1992; Villamil and Guerrero 1998). Such trained students have been found to be able to give specific responses to their peers' writing and to advise, collaborate, and point out problems with content and rhetoric (Berg 1999; Hansen 2001; Hansen and Liu 2000; Hedgcock and Lefkowitz 1992; Lockhart and Ng 1995; Mendonça and Johnson 1994; Stanley 1992; Villamil and Guerrero 1998). Analysis of the interaction in peer response groups has shown that students actively ask questions (both requests for information and comprehension checks); give and ask for explanations (of unclear points, opinion, content); restate; give suggestions; and correct grammar mistakes (Mendonça and Johnson 1994). In fact, peers may give better content feedback than teachers if the students are paired based on the same fields of study (Belcher 1990). In addition, peer response groups can be a fruitful environment for students to negotiate meaning and practice a wide range of language skills (Lockhart and Ng 1995), which are integral not only to their development as second language writers but also to the development of all four language skills—reading, writing, listening, and speaking.

Overall, it appears that while there are some justified concerns about the ability of students to give concrete feedback to their peers, if students are trained and given guidance and support, the interaction in the peer response group is useful and the comments generated can be constructive in helping students revise their drafts.

## Whose feedback do students adopt in their revisions?

When students' comments are given at the same time as those of their teacher, there is some question as to whose feedback students adopt when they revise (see chap. 5 for a detailed discussion of what students focus on during peer response). This is a very real issue, and if it is not handled well, the effects of peer response can be seriously diminished. In many instances of peer response, teachers also provide feedback on the same drafts as peers do, and students themselves self-correct as well. This poses the question of whether students do in fact utilize their peers' comments in revision or whether they rely solely on teacher- and self-generated revisions.

While some research indicates that students utilize only a small percentage of their peers' comments in revision (e.g., 5 percent for the students in Connor and Asenavage's 1994 study; see also Nelson and Murphy 1993; Partridge 1981; Tsui 1999), much of the research has shown that students utilize all three types of feedback (self-, peer, and teacher) (e.g., Caulk 1994; Chaudron 1984; Cheong 1994; Mendonça and Johnson 1994; Paulus 1999), even if at times they rely more on their teacher's feedback for revision (Cheong 1994). In fact, research on revisions based on teacher versus peer feedback has shown that both teacher and peer feedback helped students (Caulk 1994; Chaudron 1984; Paulus 1999), especially since peer feedback seemed to be more focused on specific concerns whereas teacher feedback was more general (Caulk 1994). A study comparing the revisions of one group that received teacher feedback only and one group that received peer feedback only found that there were no significant differences in revision—both groups performed equally well (Hedgcock and Lefkowitz 1992). In addition, peer feedback has also been found to encourage further revision after the peer response activities have ended (Paulus 1999; Villamil and Guerrero 1998), indicating that students continued to consider their peers' comments when revising their drafts on their own.

The fact that some studies have shown that students appear to rely mostly on feedback from teachers when it is given simultaneously with feedback from peers is not surprising—the teacher is the voice of authority on the rhetorical and grammatical conventions the students are learning and is the individual who gives the student a grade. Giving teacher feedback at the same time as peers' feedback also seems to undermine the effect of the peers' feedback, since it seems to imply that the teacher does not fully trust peers to be the sole source of feedback. There are a number of alternatives that might solve this dilemma. First, as is described in chapter 4, the teacher might be part of the peer-revision activity and serve as a peer, thereby taking on a supporting rather than an authoritative role in the peer response activities. Second, peer feedback and teacher feedback may be given on different drafts. For example, if students are encouraged to do multiple drafting, the initial feedback may be given by peers, with feedback on the second draft given by teachers, or vice versa. Finally, once peers have been instructed in how to provide peer feedback, the teacher may minimize her or his role in the revision and avoid giving feedback until the final draft.

### Does peer response lead to quality revision?

Probably the most important question we can ask about peer response concerns its effectiveness with regard to revision. Does peer response lead to quality revisions? Simply put, does it work? Are students' drafts better after undergoing peer response? Research on revision has shown that overall, both L1 and L2 writers, especially novice writers, tend to make surface revisions (Bereiter and Scardamalia 1987; Berger 1990). Additionally, writers are selective in choosing what and whose feedback they utilize in revising their drafts (Mendonça and Johnson 1994; Nelson and Murphy 1993; Villamil and Guerrero 1998). This is positive, since the goal of any writing class, and any activities within the writing class, is to help students become independent decision makers.

However, an important question remains about whether peer response leads to the quality revisions that justify the use of class time. The answer appears to be that it does. Peer response comments have been found to lead to meaningful revisions, especially if peers are trained (Berg 1999; Hansen 2001; Hansen and Liu 2000; Hedgcock and Lefkowitz 1992; Paulus 1999; Stanley 1992; Villamil and Guerrero 1998). In fact, peer revision has been found to be more effective than self-revision (Berger 1990) and equal to teacher feedback in terms of revision quality (Caulk 1994; Chaudron 1984). Furthermore, in a comparison of revisions based on peer-only versus teacher-only feedback, it was found that revisions based on peer feedback were better in content, organization, and vocabulary, while revisions based on teacher feedback were only better in grammar and mechanics (Hedgcock and Lefkowitz 1992). The interaction in the peer response groups also seems to have an effect on the extent to which comments and suggestions are incorporated into revisions—if the groups are cooperative, there appears to be more negotiated interaction and more incorporations of peer suggestions into revision (Nelson and Murphy 1993). Finally, increased text length has been found as a result of peer response, which indicates that this type of activity can affect the thinking about and restructuring of a text (Villamil and Guerrero 1998).

The effectiveness of peer response in leading to quality revisions may be explained by a number of factors. First of all, as a number of studies have shown (e.g., Caulk 1994; Connor and Asenavage 1994; Hedgcock and Lefkowitz 1992; Paulus 1999), teachers tend to focus more on grammatical concerns in giving feedback, while peers focus more on content and rhetorical concerns. Peers' comments may also at times be more specific than teachers' and thus be more effective for revision (Caulk 1994). Second, peer response allows for a negotiated interaction, which gives learners opportunities to discuss their peers' questions and come up with alternatives in their writing. Teachers' comments tend to be in written format on the draft, and students may not always understand these comments or how to make corrections based on them. While many teachers have conferences with students to discuss revision strategies, thereby giving students the opportunity to ask questions, some students may feel uncomfortable questioning the teacher's comments, since teachers are typically in an authoritative role in the classroom. Therefore, students who are revising solely on the basis of teacher feedback may be revising their texts but not really knowing why (or how) they are making the revisions. In contrast, in the peer response situation the power relationships are more balanced, and students may feel more comfortable questioning and discussing their peers' comments. In peer response situations students work with their peers in a collaborative manner; they can negotiate, agree, or even disagree with their peers' comments. In other words, while they may tend to take their teacher's comments at face value and revise without really understanding why, students may tend to engage in more negotiations with

peers regarding advice and suggestions, which ultimately benefits everyone in the group and specifically may provide the
writer with more concrete ideas to use in revision.

In summary, peer response can be effective in helping
learners develop their writing skills through interacting with
other readers/writers, reading others' work, getting others'
perspectives on their own work, and negotiating about content and rhetorical and grammatical issues. Students are able
to give specific feedback regarding content and rhetorical and
grammatical issues, which is valued and employed successfully in revision, especially if students have undergone instruction in how to respond to their peers' papers. Feedback
from peers has been found to be as effective as that from teachers in helping students revise their papers, especially in terms
of rhetorical and content issues, since these seem to be the
main focus of comments in peer response.

## Long-Term Effects: The Effects of Peer Response on Language Development

Now that we have established that peer response can be effective for the revision of students' papers, we are faced with
another question. Are the benefits of peer response short term
only (see the earlier discussion), or are there any long-term effects of peer response in terms of L2 learners' overall language
development?

As is discussed in the introduction, there are a number of
cognitive and psycholinguistic justifications for using peer response activities in the language classroom. First of all, based
on the theoretical framework of Vygotsky (1978), research on
peer-group interactions (e.g., Guerrero and Villamil 1994;
DiCamilla and Anton 1997; Donato 1994; Villamil and Guerrero 1996, 1998) has shown that collective scaffolding takes
place during the interactions in peer groups, students taking
the roles of both novice and expert as they guide each other
in completing the necessary task(s). The result of this scaffolding is that students learn from each other, and this learn-

ing can encompass not only rhetorical, content, or stylistic issues but also overall language development. Research has shown that what students learn as the result of this scaffolding may have long-term effects on their language development (Donato 1994).

Additionally, research on interaction and second language acquisition has also indicated that students need opportunities to negotiate meaning in order to develop their second language skills. Research on group work in general and peer response activities in particular has found that these types of classroom situations increase the opportunities students have to engage in negotiations and test hypotheses and also provide learners with the chance to practice a wide range of language functions, more than they would be able to in a regular teacher-led classroom. While there is a scarcity of research on the long-term benefits of peer response for writing and overall language development, the fact that research on interaction in peer response activities (e.g., Guerrero and Villamil 1994; Lockhart and Ng 1995; Villamil and Guerrero 1998) has shown that students employed a wide range of language functions and negotiated meaning during the activities does indicate that language development is taking place, even if it is not immediately apparent. For example, within peer response activities, students have been shown to scaffold each other, advise, respond to advice, elicit information, respond to elicitations, and request clarification (Villamil and Guerrero 1996). Students have also been shown to ask questions, both requests for information and comprehension checks; give and ask for explanations; restate; give suggestions; and correct grammar (Mendonça and Johnson 1994). Additionally, the language development that takes place may encompass all four language skills—reading, writing, listening, and speaking—especially in peer response modes that are both verbal and written in nature. There is also some indication that peer comments generated during peer response activities may lead to long-term benefits, while teachers' responses are more effective in terms of short-term benefits (Partridge 1981), although this issue needs more research.

## Suggestions for Teachers

Based on this discussion of the effects of peer response on students' perceptions, their revisions, and their long-term language learning, the following suggestions are offered to make peer response activities more effective.

- Instructing students in peer response is essential. Students who undergo instruction give more specific, and thus better, comments regarding content, rhetoric, and organization. Along with this, students should have a clear understanding of why they are engaging in peer response and how this will benefit their writing (see chap. 6 for a more detailed discussion of how, when, and why to instruct students in peer response).
- It may be more beneficial to use peer response and teacher response on different drafts. For example, in a process approach to writing, students write multiple drafts. The teacher may respond to the first draft and then utilize peer response for the second draft, or vice versa. An alternative would be for the teacher to give comments on the same draft as the peers do but to give these comments to the student only after the student has had the opportunity to take peers' comments into consideration.
- In order to ensure that students are considering content and rhetorical issues when reviewing each other's drafts and making specific comments for revision, teachers might model this behavior in giving feedback on their students' papers. Teachers should give students the kinds of comments on their papers that they want them to make on each other's papers.
- It is advisable that in the early stages of peer response, students use guided peer response sheets to elicit specific comments on content and rhetorical and grammatical issues (see chap. 6 for examples of questions for use in peer response). After students have become more familiar with peer response, they may not need

to use the guided sheets but instead could be asked to focus on several issues such as organization, unity, support, etc.

- It may also be beneficial to have students engage in multiple peer response activities across various drafts of the same paper. This process approach to responding fits well into a course with a process approach to writing and reinforces the different stages of the writing process. For the first draft, for example, students may be asked to focus on content and rhetorical issues. In responding to subsequent drafts, students may focus on organization/stylistic concerns and later on grammatical errors. This also fits well with the second suggestion, that students and teachers respond to different drafts—for example, students might respond to the first draft and the teacher to the second, or vice versa.

- Along with this, it is important that the students read their peers' final drafts after all revision has taken place. In fact, it may be useful to have a group reading of the final drafts so that students can see the effect of their comments on their peers' revisions and also understand why their comments were or were not utilized in revision.

- Teachers should be available during the peer response activities in order to guide and assist students in a nonauthoritative manner. Initially, it may be useful for teachers to participate in the peer response activities as a peer (see chap. 4); as students become more familiar with peer response, the teacher may only need to be available to answer questions and offer guidance and support.

- It is also important to emphasize to students that as writers they are ultimately the final decision makers regarding what should and what should not be revised. During the peer response activities, students can negotiate with their peers about suggested revisions in order to gain a deeper understanding of their peers' reading of their text. Rather than either accepting or rejecting their peers' comments, students should instead find out why the comments were made and then decide whether or not the revisions would make the paper more effective.

- Finally, students should be made responsible for critically evaluating the comments made by their peers, as well as those made by their teacher. It is the goal of a writing class—and thus of the peer response activities within the class—to make writers autonomous. Therefore, in an effort to ensure that students are critically evaluating revision comments and not accepting them at face value or rejecting them because making the revisions may be too time-consuming, students should make a list of all the comments they received (this can be done during or after the peer response session, depending on whether the groups were in oral, written, or oral plus written modes) and state whether or not they utilized them in revision and why or why not. This list can be handed in with the final draft. (A sample of a form that could be used to aid students in making such a list appears in table 15, chap. 6.)

# Chapter 2
## Contexts of Peer Response: Types of Programs and Levels of Students

This chapter explores the social context of peer response, specifically focusing on factors such as foreign versus second language settings and types of students (younger writers versus adult writers). We believe that there are a number of issues that can potentially have an impact on peer response activities, depending on the setting, the program, and the students involved in peer response. Some of these issues are: the language of peer response (L1, L2, or both); the purpose of L2 writing; the L1 and L2 literacy backgrounds of students; the teacher's linguistic and cultural background; and the participation patterns of students in whole-class and group activities. Each of these issues will be discussed under the two main sections of this chapter: Second Language versus Foreign Language Settings and Types of Students.

### Second Language versus Foreign Language Settings

To what extent does whether a setting is a second language setting or a foreign language setting have an impact on peer response? What is the nature of the impact, and why? In this discussion of peer response contexts, we will focus on four main issues that we believe have an impact on peer response and are contextually determined, to a large extent: (1) the linguistic and cultural backgrounds of teachers and learners, (2) learners' skill development, (3) class size, and (4) reasons for taking a writing course.

## The Linguistic and Cultural Backgrounds of Teachers and Learners

A number of issues related to the teacher may not be as clear-cut as they initially appear. One of these issues is whether the teacher is a native or nonnative speaker of English. While it is certainly true that most teachers of English in foreign language contexts are nonnative speakers of English and that most ESL teachers in second language contexts are native speakers, this dichotomy is simplistic, at best. As recent research on issues related to nonnative speakers of English as teachers in TESOL suggests (e.g., Kamhi-Stein 2000; Liu 1999; Samimy and Brutt-Griffler 1999), there is no simple definition of native versus nonnative speakerness; in fact, the use of the term itself is questionable, since it creates a dichotomy that implies differences in language proficiency—which is not necessarily the case—and reinforces bias in hiring practices when only native speakers are urged to apply for jobs.

Our position on this issue (both of us are nonnative speakers of English, with one of us often mislabeled as a native speaker based on language proficiency and ethnic background) is that the language status of the teacher may not in itself be a relevant issue in peer response; rather, issues of *shared linguistic and cultural backgrounds between the teacher and students appear to be more pertinent,* as these issues may have important implications for classroom participation styles and especially for norms of group work in the classroom and language use during peer response activities.

What is the impact of the teacher's and learners' linguistic background on peer response? First of all, we need to consider the possible types of contexts based on teacher and student linguistic backgrounds. In foreign language settings, the classrooms tend to be linguistically and culturally homogeneous, so a couple of classroom scenarios are typical: the teacher does share the language of her or his students (e.g., a Japanese teacher of English in Japan); or the teacher does not share the native language of the students (e.g., an English teacher from the United States teaching in Taiwan).

In second language settings, the picture becomes even more complicated, since the classroom tends to be heterogeneous, although it can be homogeneous in certain areas of the United States where there are larger concentrations of speakers of certain languages, as in the case of Spanish speakers in some Southwestern areas of the United States and in the case of special programs and classes developed for students. Therefore, in second language contexts, the following scenarios are possible: the teacher shares the native language of the students, the teacher shares the native language of some of the students, and the teacher does not share the native language of any of the students.

The linguistic and cultural backgrounds of the students also complicate these scenarios. For example, students may share the same cultural and linguistic background with each other, which is typically the case in foreign language contexts. However, as previously mentioned, this background may or may not be shared with their teacher. Students also may not share the same cultural and linguistic background, which is more often the case in second language settings. The teacher may share the background of some of the students or of none of them.

Table 3 illustrates these different scenarios, providing examples of where they are commonly found and listing the implications of each of these scenarios for language use in peer response groups and for the participation patterns of students during group work. Each of these scenarios will be discussed in detail with reference to language use and participation patterns.

These varying scenarios have implications for peer response activities in terms of what language will be used during peer response and what the norms and expectations of participation patterns are. These two issues will be discussed in detail later in the chapter.

### Language Use Issues

In settings where students share the same native language with each other and with the teacher, the language of peer re-

**TABLE 3.   Teacher and Student Scenarios across Foreign and Second Language Contexts**

| Language Context | Scenario | Language Use | Group and Class Participation Norms |
|---|---|---|---|
| Foreign and Second Language | Teacher shares L1 with students; students are homogeneous[a] | L1, L2, both | Similar norms; teacher understands students' perceptions about group work |
| | Teacher does not share L1 with students; students are homogeneous | L2 mostly; students may be L1 linguistic resource for each other | Norms may differ; teacher may have to spend more time on sociocultural issues in group work |
| Second Language | Teacher shares L1 with some students; students are heterogeneous | L2 use in groups; some learners may be linguistic resources for each other | Students may have different expectations of group work; teacher may know some potential issues |
| | Teacher does not share L1 with students; students are heterogeneous | L2 mostly | Students may have different expectations of group work from those of teacher and other students; teacher may know some potential issues through reading the literature |

[a]We are not trying to suggest that language similarities imply cultural similarities. In some cases, however, speakers of the same language background may share similar cultural expectations about classroom participation norms (e.g., speakers of Chinese from both the People's Republic of China and Taiwan).

sponse activities may be the L1, the L2, or both, while the text itself is in the L2. The variety in language choice creates several options for the language of peer response; each option has implications for language development and the focus of peer response.

If the peer response takes place in a second language classroom and the text to be responded to is in the L2, the most obvious choice is peer response in the L2 only. However, it is important to note that while the teacher can dictate which language students should use, what actually happens in the groups during peer response may be L1 use or a mixture of L1 and L2 use. The mode of peer response is an important factor. If the comments are written only or are generated via computer-mediated communications software, then students may not have as many difficulties with L2 use only. However, if peer response activities are also conducted in an oral mode, students may feel uncomfortable talking in the L2 with each other when they all share the same L1 and are only using the L2 in this setting, especially if the learners have had limited opportunities for L2 oral communication and therefore have difficulty expressing their ideas orally. (See the discussion that follows on compensating for skill-area difficulties in peer response activities.) Additionally, as stated earlier, the teacher's suggestion that peer response activities be conducted in the L2 only may not necessarily result in L2 use—it is unrealistic to expect that students in this setting will consistently employ the L2. Instead, the students may revert to the L1 as a means of more natural communication. On the other hand, the peer response session may be one of the best opportunities students have for L2 use, since they have greater opportunities to practice the L2—in other words, more chances to talk—than in full-class activities.

Another possible option is to have the students conduct the peer response activity in the L1, even though the text is written in the L2. The arguments for this option are: (a) the focus of the course is writing development in the L2, and the text has been written in the L2, so the goal has been met; (b) allowing students to employ the L1 gives them greater freedom in expressing their ideas, especially if their oral communication skills are not as strong; and (c) students are not hindered in what they say by a lack of L2 linguistic knowledge.

Conversely, however, the following problems can be created: (a) only reading and writing development in the L2 is fostered; (b) students lose a valuable opportunity for listening and speaking development; and (c) the employment of the L1 in peer response may lead to a greater focus on grammar or surface revisions, perhaps due to the literacy practices of the L1 culture (Huang 1996).

The third option is to allow students to use both languages while engaging in peer response. One method of doing this might be to explain the linguistic benefits of L2 use, especially if the regular classroom activities afford few opportunities for this, but to allow students to use the L1 as a linguistic resource when absolutely necessary. In fact, this can be done so that one of the group members has the role of a "language manager"—in other words, a person who monitors language use within the group so that students are encouraged to employ the L2 whenever possible. If a student does not know a term in the L2 then she or he could ask the group for the term in the L2 by using the L1, therefore creating opportunities for scaffolding in the L2 while still allowing for more flexible communication in the group.

If the teacher does not share the native language of the students, the students may be more encouraged to use the L2 during the peer response activities, since the teacher will not understand them if they use the L1. However, in this scenario as well, expecting L2 use only may be unrealistic. Instead, fostering an environment for L2 use and then allowing students to use the L1 as a linguistic resource when necessary may work best to meet the language objectives of the peer response activity and the linguistic needs of the students.

### Classroom Participation Issues

If the cultural backgrounds of the students are homogeneous and the teacher is an insider of the culture, a couple of scenarios are likely: (1) group work as an educational activity is a common classroom style for the teacher and students; or (2) group work is uncommon and unfamiliar to students. In either case, since the teacher is aware of the students' expectations of classroom participation and group work, she or he can anticipate the issues that can potentially arise, especially if students are unfamiliar with these participation patterns. As an insider, the teacher can engage students in discussions comparing and contrasting participation styles across cultures and the educational and linguistic benefits of group work in contrast to teacher-led activities, if they are the norm in a particular culture; this may facilitate interest in and motivate students to try group work.

If the teacher is not a member of the students' culture and the students' cultural and linguistic backgrounds are homogeneous, the following scenarios are possible: (1) the teacher is familiar with group work, but the students are not; (2) both the teacher and the students are familiar with group work; (3) neither the teacher nor the students are familiar with group work; or (4) the students are familiar with group work, but the teacher is not. If the teacher is unfamiliar with group work, this book, we hope, can give the teacher justifications for employing it in the L2 classroom, along with practical guidelines for implementing it. Therefore, the fourth scenario can be resolved (as can the third, to some extent). In terms of the second scenario, students and teachers may have different expectations about turn-taking behavior and linguistic expressions; again, educating students in group work will also necessitate discussing issues of sociocultural norms and pragmatic language in group work. The first scenario (and the third, once the teacher has become familiar with group work) is a bit more complicated. If the teacher is familiar with group work and the students are not and the teacher is not a member of the students' culture, then the teacher may not be aware of the potential issues that may arise in group work. One way to minimize problems and to facilitate group cohesion is to discuss educational patterns of group work and classroom participation in the students' and teacher's cultures and as a group come up with a list of suggestions for appropriate group work behavior so that everyone feels comfortable with the new task.

If the students' backgrounds are heterogeneous, the teacher will have to be especially sensitive to the various expectations students have about group and classroom participation patterns and turn-taking in the groups. As is discussed in chapter 6, one part of familiarizing students with peer response activities is addressing pragmatic and sociocultural aspects of intercultural communication and group work. In heterogeneous classes, misunderstandings and potential communication problems are more likely, but these can be minimized if the students explore issues such as turn-taking and appropriate linguistic expressions before commencing group work (see chap. 6). Since the teacher may share the cultural and linguistic background of some of the students, he or she may also be aware of some of the difficulties students may face in group work and thus be able to foresee and decrease any problems. Misunderstandings can be minimized if the class has discussed cultural norms for classroom behaviors and linguistic phrases that are appropriate in peer response and perhaps developed a set of guidelines for appropriate group behavior (which can encompass linguistic, pragmatic, and turn-taking behaviors) before group work commences. In fact, this type of classroom scenario provides a rich environment for learning beyond writing, as it gives learners a unique opportunity to become sensitive to cross-cultural differences and develop both metalinguistic and pragmatic knowledge.

## Learners' Skill Development

Another important issue related to foreign and second language contexts concerns the skill areas that have been focused on in each language context. In foreign language contexts, learners may have fewer opportunities for speaking and listening practice, and the focus of the curriculum may be on developing reading, writing, and grammar skills. In second language contexts, learners may have more opportunities for speaking and listening development, and oral language development may have a greater emphasis in instruction. The skills with which learners have difficulty may affect the modes of peer response (see chap. 4 for more details about modes and roles in peer response). For example, if learners have had few opportunities for oral language development, they may have difficulty expressing their ideas in an oral mode of peer response. For learners who have more difficulty with reading or writing, as may be the case for some learners who also have had limited opportunity to develop their L1 and L2 literacy skills, reading a peer's paper during a limited class period may be a difficult task. In order to address these issues and provide possible solutions and thus facilitate peer response activities, table 4 describes the four skill areas, the potential problems in each, and possible solutions.

All of these suggestions strive to promote collaborative learning and provide opportunities for scaffolding and inter-action in order to promote L2 use and negotiation of meaning. All the activities also try to facilitate development of all four language skills.

### Class Size

A third important difference between second and foreign lan-guage programs is class size. In some foreign language con-texts, for example, class size may be relatively large (e.g., 45 students in some college English classes in China), while class size may be slightly smaller in some second language contexts, depending of course on the program. Class size can affect peer response in numerous ways. First of all, teachers with larger class sizes may be hesitant to employ peer re-sponse activities in their classes because they feel that they are unable to monitor the number of groups a large class will create, especially in an activity that may necessitate monitor-ing, such as peer response. Second, if peer response activities are used, it may be challenging for teachers to monitor the progress of each group and address the individual issues that emerge during the activities. However, peer response activi-ties may be especially beneficial in such settings, since they will: (a) provide students with opportunities for second lan-guage use, which may be extremely limited in more tradi-tional, teacher-led activities; (b) be more time-efficient, since students will get feedback on their papers in a shorter amount of time than they would if the teacher had to respond to all the papers by her or himself; and (c) give students more feed-

**TABLE 4.  Skill-Area Problems and Solutions in Peer Response**

| Skill Area | Problems | Solutions |
| --- | --- | --- |
| Listening | Difficulty understanding peers | Use a written mode of peer response first and then have students look at filled-out peer response sheets while discussing comments. |
| | | Allow students to tape record the oral discussion. |
| | | Appoint one person the note-taker of the group. |
| Speaking | Difficulty articulating ideas | Give students peer response papers one day before to allow them time to write out their comments. |
| | | Give language for students to use in peer response (see chap. 6). |
| | Difficulty with pronunciation | Have students write the words they have difficulty saying. |
| Reading | Not enough time to read | Give peer response papers one day before. |
| | | Have students read their papers out loud as other students follow on the written drafts. |
| | Difficulty with vocabulary | Have students enclose a list of difficult vocabulary words and their definitions with their drafts. |
| | | Have students go over the vocabulary as a group before they read the papers or while reading the papers. |
| | Difficulty with content | Group students by content topic. |
| | | Have students meet before reading peers' papers and give background information on topics to help schemata development. |
| Writing | Not enough time to write comments while reading others' drafts | Give drafts to students the night before or one class day before to give them sufficient time to respond on drafts. |
| | Not enough time to write comments of peers on own draft | Let students use L1 if it facilitates note-taking. |
| | Difficulty with English orthography | Have a peer help student write out difficult words. |

back on their papers than they might otherwise receive due to the number of students in class.

Peer response can be effectively employed in classes of all sizes. In order to ensure that peer response is effective, we suggest the following.

- Assign roles to each participant to ensure that each is participating in the peer response activity and that the peer response is clearly structured. These roles might be: timekeeper, note-taker, writer, and solicitor of comments.
- Provide clear guidelines for peer response, including guidelines for time, roles, and comments.
- Have students read the papers the day before so that time in class can be more effectively used for peer response activities.
- If possible, conduct out-of-class peer response sessions with the instructor (see chap. 4) the first time to model peer response behavior and give individual attention to each student's questions and concerns, and/or work with each group of four after class for 20 minutes or so until all groups have met with the instructor. Subsequent peer response activities can then be conducted in class.
- If this is not possible, or to provide further peer response modeling, show videotapes of and/or simulate an exemplary peer response group and a mediocre peer response group. (These can be scripted out beforehand, and students can volunteer to play the different roles.) Then discuss what went wrong and what was successful.
- On a rotating basis, have the members of one group (and of a different group the next time, and so on) serve as assistants to help you monitor peer response activities and address any questions that come up. These assistants can each monitor one or two groups, as needed, and also serve as timekeepers to ensure that students get through all the papers as predetermined by class time.

### Reasons for Being in the Writing Course

Finally, the reasons behind students' enrollment in the writing course may also vary widely across contexts and may be markedly different in foreign and second language contexts. In foreign language contexts, students studying writing in English may be working on developing their English writing skills in order to pass English language requirements both at the secondary and postsecondary levels. Some of these students may also be taking the Test of English as a Foreign Language (TOEFL) in order to enter universities for academic study, and as the computerized version of the TOEFL automatically includes writing, students may be practicing their writing skills in order to pass that test. Therefore, in many foreign language contexts, English language writing appears to be heavily test-oriented. However, in these contexts, other types of writing may also be necessary, such as business and technical writing, writing for academia, and writing focusing on personal expression. Communication through E-mail is also becoming increasingly important, thus establishing another need for English writing development. In many cases, the need to communicate in English via writing may not be as immediate as in a second language setting, and therefore motivation may differ in terms of investment in writing development. In second language contexts, writing may serve a more immediate need and in fact be required across academic, work, and social settings. For these reasons, the type of writing that is required in second language contexts may be wider in range.

The purpose of writing may have an effect on peer response in several ways. First of all, the genre or type of writing may differ according to context; therefore, peer response activities in second language contexts may take place across a wider array of writing genres. The implication of this is that students will need to be exposed to more examples of rhetorical patterns. Thus, teachers may need to create a wider variety of peer response sheets in order to address the varying rhetorical patterns. In foreign language contexts, where the range of writing genres students will be expected to learn may also vary widely, students may not have as many opportunities for exposure to different rhetorical forms, especially in authentic materials. Therefore, in this setting, one focus of peer response may be on rhetorical patterns. Second, students may have varying attitudes toward peer response in the classroom. If students are studying second language writing in order to pass writing requirements, they may find little value in engaging in peer response activities. However, across settings and varying purposes for writing, students can be made aware of the benefits of peer response if teachers discuss how peer response can be viewed as a scaffolding activity for self-revision at later stages. In other words, through collaborative negotiation with peers, students may develop greater grammatical and rhetorical awareness that can help them when they need to do self-revision—for example, during a writing test.

## Types of Students

This discussion will focus on younger and adult writers. Issues relevant in terms of the implementation of peer response activities will be discussed with relation to each of these two populations of writers.

### Younger Writers

Younger writers can be defined as students in primary, middle, and (to some extent) secondary education. These younger writers may be mainstreamed in the school system and receive little to no ESL instruction or be placed in one of the following types of programs: Sheltered Instruction/Specially Designed Academic Instruction in English (SISDAIE), ESL Pullout, English Language Development (ELD), English as a Foreign Language, Transitional Bilingual Education, Maintenance Bilingual Education, Immersion Education, and Two-Way Immersion. Each of these programs will be briefly described.

- *Sheltered Instruction/Specially Designed Academic Instruction in English* (SISDAIE) is content-based instruction specifically designed to facilitate the English language development of ESL students. These programs are usually aimed at intermediate or advanced students.
- *ESL Pullout* programs feature students who are usually mainstreamed for the majority of classroom instruction and then pulled out for special ESL instruction on a regular basis.
- *English Language Development* (ELD) is content-based instruction by teachers specifically trained in second language development issues. Students are instructed in English language and literacy, as well as in all subject areas.
- *English as a Foreign Language* (EFL) is English instruction in foreign language contexts when English is the subject matter.
- *Transitional Bilingual Education* programs help students mainstream to classes as quickly as possible by providing them with primary language instruction for one to three years so that they develop the literacy skills and content knowledge necessary to facilitate transition.
- *Maintenance Bilingual Education* is designed to maintain learners' primary language and develop their English language skills. Instruction in the primary language is provided through all primary and secondary levels in some cases.
- *Two-Way Immersion* is dual language instruction for English language learners and native speakers of English, focused on developing bilingualism in all students. The non-English language may be used in the early grades, and English language instruction may increase in time as the grade levels increase. (For a fuller description of ELD, Bilingual Education, and Immersion programs, see Peregoy and Boyle 2001.)

While there are notable differences among these programs in terms of their goals (English language development or bilingual language development), the length of time each takes (a few months to several years), and in-class time spent on English language development, the issues teachers may face in terms of implementing peer response activities with younger learners are similar to some extent. We believe the following issues are pertinent in implementing peer response activities with younger learners: L1 and L2 literacy development, grouping, length of peer response activities, and the focus of peer response. Each of these issues will be explored.

### L1 and L2 Literacy Development

Both first and second language literacy development may be particularly important for younger learners, especially in second language contexts, in which primary language development is not easily maintained. As Collier (1987) posits, while it takes ESL students approximately two to three years to develop basic intercultural communication skills (BICS), it may take these same students five to seven years to develop academic literacy skills in English if they are already literate in their first language and possibly seven to nine years if they are not literate in their first language. This means that for the most part, students in K–12 (as well as adult learners, of course) are still in the process of developing literacy skills in English, even if their oral communication skills appear quite strong. As research indicates, students who are literate in their first languages have an advantage in second language development, as strategies for L1 reading and writing and knowledge about the functions and forms of reading and writing appear to transfer to L2 writing and reading (Cummins 1981; Peregoy 1989). Similarities between orthographic conventions may also help students develop L2 literacy skills more rapidly (Odlin 1989). However, differences in these conventions, as well as in rhetorical patterns, may create difficulties for students in developing literacy skills in English (Odlin 1989). In contrast, if students have had few experiences with written literacy practices and have not had experience in reading and writing in their native language, English literacy development may take more time. The implication for peer response activities is that learners may be at different stages of literacy development (e.g., some learners may be struggling with the orthographic conventions of English—employing invented spellings, which is in fact a sign that they are making progress in learning English spelling rules—while others may be good spellers but struggling with other writing issues) and that therefore peer response activities may need to be flexible across groups (i.e., that different groups need to work on different aspects of writing) and the school year, as learners may have differential rates in acquiring literary skills in academic English. No one focus for peer response may fit all students.

### Grouping

Group size is an especially important issue with younger learners (see chap. 3 for a description of other issues involved in grouping students). It is probably more efficient to create pairs or groups of three for younger learners in order to provide the activity with more structure and monitor the learners more closely. In addition, as learners are likely to be at different proficiency levels in the classroom, heterogeneous groups may work well, since classrooms are rich environments for collaborative learning activities and peer/teacher scaffolding.

### Length of Peer Response Activities

Shorter activities may be more appropriate for younger learners and for learners who are in the beginning stages of literacy development. While peer response activities for older learners (including high-schoolers) can stretch across several class periods, with approximately 20 to 30 minutes allotted to each student's paper, activities for younger learners need to be developed that keep their shorter attention spans in mind. Therefore smaller groups are encouraged, as stated earlier, with 10 minutes or so spent on each paper, so that peer response activities last for less than 30 minutes or so per session.

### Focus of Peer Response

As is described earlier, since students in this population of learners may still be in the process of developing English literacy skills and since there is likely to be great variety in literacy development among these groups of learners, especially in second language contexts, the focus of peer response activities may need to be flexible. In spite of the great variation in proficiency levels for this group of learners, and perhaps because of it, peer response activities can be an especially fruitful way of fostering language development because of the scaffolding that occurs through this type of collaborative learning activity. In fact, as prior research on peer response groups with younger ESL learners has shown, peer response is an extremely important activity in the classroom, since it helps students share personal experiences (Samway 1987; Urzúa 1987). This type of activity is certainly important in all language classrooms, since it fosters supportive learning environments and a friendly atmosphere; it may be especially important in classrooms in which students have been mainstreamed with regular students in order to create supportive bonds in those classrooms as well. In terms of younger students' abilities to provide peer support in writing, studies have also shown that young ESL learners can give each other cooperative assistance regarding both content and rhetorical matters (Samway 1987; Urzúa 1987), as well as grammatical matters (Peregoy and Boyle 1990). Therefore, it is possible to have students focus on all three areas—content, rhetoric, and grammar—but it may be necessary to be flexible across learners in terms of what to focus on and when. This gives the teacher several options.

- Students may benefit, at least initially, from writing about more personal experiences, since they have the background knowledge (i.e., the content schemata) and may be more successful approaching something about which they have personal knowledge.

- Peer response forms (which will necessarily be briefer with younger students and lower-proficiency learners) can be tailored to focus on the specific individual problems of students.
- Students can create their own peer response forms (or sets of three to four questions) that address the issues they want to ask their peers about in order to improve their writing (e.g., "Do I need more adjectives to talk about my dog?").
- The teacher can work individually with some students to create these forms, or students can create forms as groups, focusing on questions they think are important for this writing assignment.
- If the class has students at diverse stages of literacy development, teachers can develop peer-tutoring groups, in which students who have mastered an area of writing (e.g., orthographic conventions) can tutor students who have difficulty in this area.
- The teacher should create peer response forms that focus only on a few issues that are manageable for the students. Students can focus on rhetorical issues (e.g., "Does the story have an ending?"); content issues (e.g., "Is it clear why the writer was sad?"), or grammatical/stylistic issues (e.g., "Does the writer capitalize the first letter of new sentences?"). Students may focus on content and rhetorical issues after the first draft and on grammatical/stylistic issues on subsequent drafts.
- It may be helpful for the teacher to give a minilesson on a grammatical/stylistic issue and then have the students focus on this issue in their peer response during the editing stage (Peregoy and Boyle 2001).

While students can focus on all three issues across the writing of one paper, it may be best to focus on only one or two types of issues for each peer response activity. Table 5 shows examples of questions that can guide peer response activities

**TABLE 5.   Guiding Questions for Peer Response with Younger Writers**

|  | Primary Level | Middle School Level | Secondary Level |
|---|---|---|---|
| Content | What part of the story did you like the best? Why? | What interested you the most in the story? | What part of the story was the most vivid to you? Why? |
|  | What part of the story didn't you understand? | What part of the story did you want the writer to add more details to? | What part of the story needed more details and/or action? |
| Rhetoric | Did the story have an ending? | What is the climax of the story? Does the action lead up to the climax? How? | Who was the narrator of the story? Did you get a clear idea of how the narrator felt about the events in the story? |
| Grammar/Style | Are all the words spelled correctly? Are the first words in every sentence capitalized? | Are there any spelling errors in the paper? Any grammar errors? Please circle any misspelled words and underline any grammatical errors. | Are there any spelling errors in the paper? Any grammar errors? Please circle any misspelled words and underline any grammatical errors. |

across all grade levels and foci. Of course, grade level does not necessarily equate with language proficiency; however, the questions may serve as indicators of the complexity of writing that can be expected at the different grade levels. For the three grade levels—primary, middle, and secondary—the writing genre of narrative is employed, as this is a common rhetorical pattern across grade levels.

## Adult Writers

Issues surrounding the implementation of peer response activities with adult learners may overlap, to some extent, with those concerning younger learners, especially for adults with few prior literacy experiences in their L1. However, there are also a number of important differences that warrant separate treatment of this population. Adult learners may be enrolled in the following types of programs: EFL subject courses, adult literacy programs, intensive English programs (IEPs), community college programs, postmatriculation university ESL composition programs for both undergraduate and graduate students, and sections of freshman composition courses that have ESL students.

The central issues in employing peer response with adult learners are focused on L1 and L2 literacy development and on levels of proficiency. Each of these will be addressed separately.

### L1 and L2 Literacy Development

While adult learners, for the most part, tend to have more highly developed L1 literacy skills than many younger learners, there is still great variance among adult learners in terms of both L1 and L2 literacy development. Learners can be grouped into several categories: (1) developing L2 literacy skills—not literate in the L1; (2) literate in the L1—developing L2 literacy skills; (3) literate in both the L1 and the L2—developing advanced academic literacy skills.

*1. Developing L2 literacy skills—not literate in the L1.* As with some younger learners in second language contexts, some adults may not have had the opportunity to develop written literacy skills in their native language and therefore have special needs in the L2 writing classroom. Such learners are typically enrolled in adult literacy programs, which are specially designed for this population of learners. As the discussion of younger learners suggests, learners who are not literate in their L1 may have special instructional needs (e.g., exposure to different types and functions of literacy and print media, meaning-embedded practice in orthographic conventions), and levels of literacy development may vary greatly within one course. As these instructional needs are similar to those discussed for younger learners, the reader is encouraged to look at the section on younger learners for suggestions on implementing peer response activities with this population of learners.

*2. Literate in the L1—developing L2 literacy skills.* This population of adult learners is probably the most widely known in both foreign and second language contexts. These adult learners may be enrolled in a variety of programs, such as community colleges, IEPs, community- and church-based programs, EFL/ESL subject-matter courses, university post-matriculation ESL writing courses for both undergraduate and graduate students, and special sections of freshman composition courses in higher education. These students—though varying greatly in terms of purpose for English study, length of English study, and purpose for writing (i.e., genre)—share the general characteristic of being literate in their first language. This does have implications for L2 writing instruction, and therefore peer response activities, in that cross-linguistic differences and similarities in terms of rhetorical patterns, orthographic systems, grammatical patterns, vocabulary, reading and writing strategies, and culturally specific rules about the ownership of knowledge (i.e., issues of copying, paraphrasing, and plagiarism) can affect what and how these L2 writers write and thus how they are read and reviewed (Connor 1996; Odlin 1989).

For these writers, peer response activities, especially when students are grouped heterogeneously (see chap. 3), serve as excellent consciousness-raising activities about English rhetorical and grammatical patterns because of the opportunity for cross-linguistic (and cross-cultural) discussions of these issues. Through reading their peers' papers and commenting on issues such as rhetoric and grammar (see chap. 5 for a more detailed discussion of different foci), students may become more aware of how their L1 literacies shape their L2 literacy development, not just in terms of how they write but also of how they read. This, in turn, can help them become more aware of audience expectations for English writing across genres and develop English as an additional literacy without sublimating or negating the literacy characteristics of their L1.

*3. Literate in the L1 and the L2—developing advanced academic literacy skills.* This third population of learners includes advanced undergraduate and graduate writers in higher education, as well as advanced writers developing specialized literacy skills in business, medical, technical, and academic fields. These learners are characterized by highly developed literacies in both their native and second language and by their purpose for writing, which is typically work-related and addressed to other members of their respective discourse communities. The focus of their writing is therefore highly specialized, so content issues become relevant to the L2 writing classroom and therefore to peer response activities.

These students may be enrolled in English for Academic Purposes (EAP) courses, which are specifically designed to help such writers enter and become proficient in the respective discourse communities of their fields (Belcher and Braine 1995). Therefore, the types of writing tasks the students engage in may be field-specific. The content is also highly specialized and field-specific. This has several implications for the implementation of peer response activities. First of all, students may not always be familiar with the content of their peers' papers and therefore may have difficulty in responding to questions about content in the peer response process. Second, field-specific jargon, acronyms, shared knowledge, and even rhetorical patterns may also create barriers for students in gaining access to their peers' texts and in understanding them well enough to give meaningful feedback for revision. This suggests that peer response activities may be difficult to employ for this population of learners. To some extent, this may be true, in that peer response activities for this group of students may necessitate more teacher and student preparation. If well prepared, however, peer response activities can offer the same benefits for this group of learners as for others. Additionally, such activities can help them further explore the discourse conventions of their fields and clarify their own content knowledge. Finally, these activities promote collaborative learning and scaffolding and therefore can facilitate language development across all four skill areas.

The following suggestions are made to help teachers implement peer response activities for highly literate learners writing for their specific discourse communities.

- Students can be grouped according to field of study or alternatively by type of field (e.g., education, natural science, social science) in order to build on similarities between content and rhetorical knowledge.
- Students can stay in the same peer response groups across a semester so that they gradually become more familiar with the group members' subject matter and rhetorical patterns.
- Before peer response activities commence, students can get into their peer response groups (ideally a class day before they read each other's papers, to allow sufficient time) and give background information on the topic—in other words, explain it in more general terms.
- Along with this, students can teach each other the rhetorical patterns they are employing (e.g., the first project in the writing course can be for students to investigate the rhetorical conventions of their field and develop a guide sheet and then create lists of common terms), as well as the field-specific vocabulary the readers are likely to encounter in their papers. Vocabulary lists can be made and handed out along with the papers.

## Levels of Proficiency

The final section of this chapter addresses the issue of learners' levels of proficiency. While this issue has been tentatively explored elsewhere in this chapter, it is important to discuss a number of key points related to proficiency. First of all, while we tend to label learners in terms of proficiency as beginning, intermediate, or advanced (or in some programs where more course levels are possible, as low-beginner, mid-beginner, and high-beginner, and so on across the three main proficiency levels), it is important to note that proficiency level is not discrete but is a continuum—which means that learners within an intermediate class may actually be mid- and high-beginners to low-advanced—and that proficiency levels across skill areas are not uniform. Since the common proficiency-testing instruments, such as the TOEFL, the

TOEFL Essay, and the Michigan Test, focus on reading and writing, among other skill areas, and the subareas of vocabulary and grammar, students labeled as beginners based on these tests may not necessarily be beginners in terms of oral language development, etc. Of course, the validity of employing these tests for placement purposes is another important concern, albeit one that will not be addressed here.

The implications of these issues for peer response activities are as follows.

- Students may be at different levels of writing development within one writing course and therefore have different areas of difficulty in writing. As a result, there may need to be some variety in terms of the focus of peer response even within one class.
- Along with this, students may have different levels of development across the four skill areas. This means that some students may have difficulties communicating their ideas orally, while others may have difficulties listening to and understanding their peers' comments. These issues are dealt with in more detail earlier in this chapter.

Given these differences, it is still feasible (in fact highly facilitative, in terms of collaborative learning, scaffolding, and negotiation of meaning) to employ peer response activities across all proficiency levels. Additionally, as will be discussed in greater detail in chapter 5, students at all age and proficiency levels can engage in peer response activities across all foci, whether content, rhetoric, grammar, or a combination of these.

## Suggestions for Teachers

- Assess the linguistic and cognitive needs of students in terms of L1/L2 use before developing criteria for language use. L2 use only may not be feasible or effective in all language settings.

- Discuss classroom participation norms and expectations for peer response activities to address cross-cultural differences in participation norms.
- Be aware of students' possible language limitations in some skill areas and provide alternative strategies to help compensate for any problems (see table 4).
- Especially in larger classes, but also for smaller groups, clearly structure peer response by assigning roles to each participant. Roles might be: timekeeper, note-taker, writer, and solicitor of comments.
- Be sure to provide clear guidelines for timekeeping, the various roles in peer response, and commenting.
- If necessary due to time and language limitations, have students read the papers the day before so that time in class can be more effectively used for peer response activities.
- Conduct initial out-of-class training sessions with the instructor to model peer response behavior and give individual attention to each student's questions and concerns (see chap. 4).
- In larger classes, assign students on a rotating basis to serve as assistants to help the teacher monitor peer response activities of other groups and address any questions that come up.
- Be flexible in creating various peer response sheets across tasks to meet the needs of students writing for different purposes.
- For peer response with younger learners, place students in smaller groups (two to three students) and give shorter peer response tasks (of 10 to15 minutes).
- In classes with greater variance in skill area and literacy development, the foci of peer response may need to be individualized. Teachers, along with individuals or groups of students, can create flexible peer response sheets to meet the needs of individual students (see chap. 6).

- Use peer-tutoring groups to meet different areas of need (e.g., a more experienced peer may serve as a tutor to a group needing work on orthographic conventions).
- Especially for younger and/or beginning writers, teachers may need to develop minilessons on specific content-based, rhetorical, and/or grammatical issues in order to provide concrete information before students begin peer response (e.g., a minilesson on commas if this is one of the areas students will focus on in the peer response session).
- For more advanced writers, it may be necessary to group students by discipline or area if they are engaging in field-specific writing.
- Additionally, students may need to stay in the same peer response groups across the semester in order to keep building on their knowledge of their group members' writing genres, topics, and language.
- Finally, students can write vocabulary lists of field-specific terms they are using in their writing and distribute/discuss these terms prior to the reading of their papers. It may also be useful to have students discuss the topics of their papers before any reading takes place so that responders can build content-area knowledge.

# Chapter 3
## Grouping Students in Peer Response

Interaction among students in any L2 writing classroom takes place at several levels: within the individual (intrapersonal processes), between two individuals (dyadic processes or dyadic relations), among members of a group (group dynamics), and between groups (intergroup dynamics). While it is important to understand what is going on in a writing classroom at all these levels, the focus of this chapter is on individual members within a group. We will address three central questions: (1) What is a group? (2) How is a group formed? and (3) How do we sustain group work? We believe these are the fundamental issues L2 writing teachers should be familiar with when they build peer response activities into their syllabi and daily classes.

### Definition of a Group

We all know what a group is and what a group means to the people within one and the people outside. We all have experiences of group work, and we are all affiliated with more than one group, at school and in society. Group affiliations are a "universal feature of human life, and a large proportion of human behavior occurs in groups" (Ehrman and Dörnyei 1998, 71). A group is, according to Bertcher (1979, 14), "a dynamic social entity composed of two or more individuals, interacting independently in relation to one or more common goals that are valued by its members, so that each member influences and is influenced by each other, to some degree, through face to face communication." Shaw (1981, 8) concurs that a group consists of "two or more persons who are interacting with one another in such a manner that each person influences and is influenced by each other person." Going a bit further to identify two different kinds of memberships, L. Brown (1991, 3–4) posits that a group is "a small face-to-face collection of persons who interact to accomplish some purpose. The group will meet for one or more sessions, have open ended membership (where people come and go as they see fit) or closed membership (where people are constrained to attend for a specified time), and are either time limited (with time in hours and the number of meetings usually specified) or time unlimited (without a definite ending time or date)." In a similar vein, Zastrow (1989, 7) defines a group as "a plurality of individuals who are in contact with one another, who take one another into account, and who are aware of some significant commonality. An essential feature of a group is that its members have something in common and that they believe that what they have in common makes a difference."

Admittedly, these definitions of a group are a bit simplistic. Beyond this superficial level there lies some complexity in understanding the social, psychological, and physiological aspects of a group. The group is a social and psychological entity. A key characteristic of groups is social interaction (Goffman 1985). As argued by some researchers (e.g., Forsyth 1990; Lewin 1948; Shaw 1981), the definition of a group should also include some relationship dimension among the participants as no group can be formed if the interactors do not have an impact on each other or if there is no interdependence among them. Therefore, a group is "three or more interdependent individuals who influence one another through focused social interaction" (Ehrman and Dörnyei 1998, 71).

We all have worked in groups where trust, respect, and understanding reigned most of the time, and most of us, if not all, have also worked in groups where the members did not get along or did not feel comfortable working together. As L2 writing teachers, we often wonder why some peer response groups work so effectively and harmoniously together, while others tend to have frequent disputes and conflicts over many issues when their members attempt to come to an agreement.

There are numerous variables that make groups work or impede effective group functioning. But first, we need to discuss a fundamental issue—the formation of a group.

## Group Formation

How is a group formed? The formation of a group is a very complex issue. Sometimes groups are formed based on individual and social needs, and sometimes groups are assigned either purposefully or randomly by teachers. On other occasions, groups emerge because of seating proximity or convenience. Some groups have stability, as students establish a pattern for working together and develop trust, and some groups might only last for a short period of time, as some members depart while others join in.

However, when groups are initially formed, group members usually go through an exploratory process of tentative orientation, hesitant participation, and a search for meaning (Forsyth 1990; McCollom 1990). The guardedness and general anxiety characterizing early group behavior are very understandable because of the uncertainty when groups emerge. For instance, students in a newly assigned peer response group might not know what membership in a group will entail or whether they will get along with or like their peers in the group, and they may be uncertain of group members' acceptance and respect. It is not uncommon for students in a new peer response group to observe each other carefully, check out each other's language skills and communicative competence, search for viable roles for themselves in the group, and try to view themselves against other group members to determine who might be potential group leaders. Students in peer response groups might have different strategies in coping with newly formed groups. Some students might work hard to establish warm and friendly relationships with others, and some might seek opportunities to demonstrate leadership skills, while others might sit back and listen with minimal participation. These different attitudes and behaviors are related to a number of variables that we need to consider when forming groups, such as social attraction, group size, gender and age, heterogeneous versus homogeneous groups, and tensions that might arise in forming groups.

## Social Attraction

When students are asked to form their own peer response groups, we often notice that those who know each other well are likely to become members of the same group for not only the affect (comfort level and free from anxiety) but also the desire to be accepted as in-group members. Needless to say, we all have a tendency to like people who are similar to us in one way or another, and we also tend to feel similar to those whom we like. Social attraction can come from perceived similarities, proximity, and emotional ambience. Sometimes similar backgrounds, attitudes, or viewpoints will be likely to promote affiliative feelings (Deutsch 1962). Social identification theory (e.g., Hogg and Abrams 1988) also suggests that we acquire a sense of similarity through shared group memberships. When it comes to forming peer response groups in a class, students who know each other will probably agree to be in the same group before they accept or invite students whom they do not know well to join them. Oftentimes, we notice that students with similar linguistic and cultural backgrounds will show a strong preference to be in the same group for peer support. But once such homogeneous groups are formed in an ESL composition class, their members will tend to share their comments and suggestions in their native language, which the teacher might not wish to happen. Therefore, the teacher may want to deliberately encourage students to be in groups with individuals coming from different linguistic backgrounds.

## Group Size

As we have explained, a group in its clearest terms is usually made up of three or more interdependent individuals who influence one another through focused social interaction, such as in peer response activities. The size of a group is a variable that could affect any group work. Groups vary a great deal by size, and research findings on the effects of size on the efficacy of group work are inconclusive. Shaw (1981) posits that with certain types of tasks, such as brainstorming, an increase is size actually increases efficiency because of the increased range of abilities, knowledge, experience, and skills available. Another advantage of working in bigger groups is that bigger groups tend to offer greater opportunities for social interaction and are relatively easier for teachers to manage in class than small groups.

However, some research has shown that increasing the size of a group has negative repercussions on its dynamics. For instance, Wheelan and McKeage (1993) posit that larger groups tend to be characterized by increased interpersonal conflict and are prone to subgrouping and clique formation. Part of the reason is that the more people in the group, the harder it is for them to know each other well. In bigger groups, there also exists greater physical distance among group members, decreasing the amount of attention they can get from any one member and thus making it hard to have close relationships among group members (MacLennan and Dies 1992).

Based on the findings of a peer response study in an ESL composition class for graduate students at a large Midwestern U.S. university, Liu (1998) concludes that a group of three works best among various group formations, such as groups of four, five, or six. One reason, as pointed out by a student in an interview, is that students in larger groups tended to go through each other's papers merely at the surface level, leaving much explanation and justification underdeveloped and thus making peer response less effective when it came to revision because students whose papers were critiqued did not get a sense of why they needed to change certain things mentioned by their peers. As a teacher researcher, Liu (1998) also observed decreased member involvement and participation and decreased cohesiveness and task motivation among students in larger groups.

Another very important issue is that with larger groups,

those students who are not confident in their communicative competence and those who are very shy are usually left out, as there are not enough opportunities for those who need more time to contribute to the discussion as there are for those who are very outspoken. This phenomenon of uneven participation was observed by Shaw (1981) and confirmed by Liu (1998, 2000). Shaw points out that with an increase in group size, the distribution of member participation becomes increasingly uneven; in larger groups, differences between the most active group members and others persist, which results in a few students beginning to dominate and others becoming reticent. This imbalance in participation could also be explained by increased diffusion of responsibility and decreased identifiability, since students know that someone else will talk anyway, thus decreasing the motivation level of some group members who are not good at turn-taking and who will not be held accountable in the same way as when they are working in smaller groups and their lack of participation is more obvious. When we deal with ESL learners from diverse linguistic and cultural backgrounds, the different cultural interpretations of participation can also become a factor in group work (Liu 2000).

In summary, the size of a group should depend on the nature of the task, the time allowed for the task, the proficiency levels and maturity of the students, and a number of other variables. In peer response activities, however, smaller size is preferable, since students in small groups of three or four can actually go through each other's papers and examine issues of organization, rhetoric, grammar, and style in a detailed and more careful manner.

### Gender and Age

Both gender and age are pivotal in language learning, but they are less of an issue in peer response activities. For instance, a group of three women engaging in peer response is not much different from a group of three men or from any other mixed combination, as far as group dynamics are concerned. Gender does not play a substantial role in differentiating a good peer response interaction from a not so good one.

Age, on the other hand, is more important, since it marks learners at different stages, such as elementary school children, high school students, college students, and graduate students. In a way, age marks different stages in an individual's psychological development, intellectual maturity, and experience of school and society. In peer response activities, for instance, high school students might need different sets of guidelines than graduate students with regard to modes of peer response (see chap. 4), foci of peer response (see chap. 5), and instruction (see chap. 6).

Age is important when the L2 writing teacher decides how much time should be allocated for certain peer response activities. For younger children, whose attention spans are relatively shorter, peer response sessions should be short, while older students should be allowed more time to discuss issues and negotiate meaning. Additionally, with younger children, groups should be kept relatively smaller. Mature adult learners, on the other hand, might appreciate comments from many different angles and might need more confirmation and challenges in order to be convinced.

Sometimes, the age of participants appears to be confounded with gender issues. According to Levine and Moreland (1990), younger children show a marked preference for same-gender playmates, and such gender segregation persists during adolescence. However, research on gender and age has not reached any conclusions about whether there are generalizable patterns or scientific formulas for what mixture might lead to more group harmony or optimal participation. Furthermore, we cannot talk about gender without talking about the diverse linguistic and cultural backgrounds of our students. In peer response groups in ESL settings, for instance, we are dealing with learners who have brought with them their own cultural beliefs and habits, which could be totally different from those of other group members. Therefore, we also need to look into issues of heterogeneous group dynamics.

### Heterogeneous versus Homogeneous Groups

There are many ways to differentiate a heterogeneous group from a homogeneous group. One way is to look at the differences in the students' characteristics—their interests, attitudes, personalities, abilities, competence, and proficiency levels. Heterogeneous and homogeneous groups can also be distinguished by the setting in which the language is learned. In most EFL settings, L2 writing students are homogeneous in language and culture: they have most probably been raised in the same cultural environment, and they share the same native language. In most ESL settings, on the other hand, L2 writing students do not have the same linguistic or cultural backgrounds. Consequently, the communication patterns in peer response groups will bear some differences.

Homogeneity is highly valued by students, and naturally occurring groups tend to be fairly homogeneous, both because of members' self-selection and because of the departure of marginal members who do not fit the group. If a group sustains membership over a period of time, there must be something that holds everyone together. Such togetherness is a reflection of a certain type or level of homogeneity. In L2 writing classrooms, however, whether in ESL or EFL settings, learners' proficiency levels are always different in various skill areas. Therefore, on close examination, no language classroom is purely homogeneous, although EFL classrooms tend to have more homogeneity than ESL classrooms.

Dealing with heterogeneity presents a challenge for L2 writing teachers, especially in forming peer response groups. Purposefully mixing students with different linguistic abilities is a commonly practiced option and could benefit weaker students, but at the same time it could make stronger students wonder what they can get out of peer response activities.

When we deal with college students or graduate students in peer response, students' majors also become a point of distinction between homogeneous and heterogeneous groups. If all students in a group are from the same major (e.g., engineering), they might have more to share and comment on, if a paper's content is field-specific. However, if the students in a group are from different majors and these majors do not share a ground for discussion, peer response might either become very superficial or create conflicts when comments are given and received (Liu 1998).

In summary, no L2 writing group is purely homogeneous in nature. Taking into consideration different levels of hetero-geneity in group formation and purposefully building on them in forming groups might be one practical and useful way to maximize the effect of peer response activities in L2 writing classrooms.

### Tensions of Group Formation

Forming groups is not stress-free. Multiple tensions exist between individual autonomy and fusion with the group. The first tension is between the need for individuals to adjust to the group and the need for the group simultaneously to adjust to its individual members. To ease this tension, students need to negotiate their own identities with other group members. The second tension is between the need to be fully engaged in the experience of the group and the ability to be detached enough to observe the group and take corrective action on its behalf. The third tension arises because while each member of a group needs to develop his or her group connections for full individuation, the group, in order to be complete, requires that its members contribute as individuals. The fourth tension concerns boundaries. While clear boundaries around a group make it possible for its members to determine and ac-complish its work, they also take away other possibilities, such as being part of some other groups in class.

All these tensions are related to the conflict between the maintenance of individual identity and assimilation as a member of a group. Understanding these tensions and work-ing toward balancing them are important for the successful completion of peer response tasks. Writing teachers should be sensitive toward these different types of tensions, which oc-cur at different stages of peer response activities with each individual member of a group, and help students cope with them. For instance, the teacher might notice that some students are not working well with a group or that a group's members are ignoring an individual who does not seem to fit. Whatever odd situation occurs, the teacher should try to understand the nature of the problem by talking with the students, working to understand what caused it, and making suggestions for improvement. Sometimes, tensions are connected, and a lack of motivation at the beginning could affect all later stages of peer response. A sensitive teacher is one who can discover irregular and abnormal phenomena and try to work on them by observing group interaction; talking with individual students; and, if necessary, altering grouping.

## Sustaining Group Work

How do we sustain group work? How do our students work with their peers in groups? How do learners from diverse linguistic and cultural backgrounds understand each other and work together? Are there certain patterns that can be found in group development? What are some of the potential problems in group work? These questions will guide the following discussion.

One classic description of group work is characterized by five stages in the life cycle of groups (Watson, Vallee, and Mulford 1980). These are: forming, storming, norming, performing, and mourning/reforming. *Forming* is the first stage in the life cycle of groups, when members are concerned with getting to know each other as they establish the group's task. *Storming* is characterized by conflict and struggle among members over who holds the power. *Norming* is characterized by a sense of "togetherness," as group cohesion emerges. *Performing* is the stage when members often demonstrate a high level of commitment to the group. Finally, *mourning/reforming* occurs when the group realizes its existence will soon end; members may need support in disengaging from the group.

Although this five-stage description of the life cycle of groups depicts the developmental sequence of a group from start to finish, there are many groups in which sequential elements of this model do not occur. Even when all these stages occur, the pace, the rhythm, and the progress within each stage might be totally different from one group to another. For instance, in ESL settings, one peer response group might need more time for trust to develop among all the group members because they are from totally different cultural backgrounds and their views toward peer response might vary radically. Another group might spend more time negotiating the meanings of response because of linguistic difficulties. While it is hard to predict whether newly formed groups can work well from the start because of so many uncertainties and variables, there are a number of issues we believe can have an impact on the quality of group work.

### Getting Acquainted

In any kind of group work, there is an initial period in which students coming from different countries, schools/universities, departments, or majors come to terms with the fact that they are in a group with others and will have to spend some time together in an ESL or EFL class. One concern many ESL students have, for instance, is whether they belong in a group consisting of students from such diverse cultural and linguistic backgrounds. They will probably ask themselves certain questions. Am I able to speak well so that other group members can understand me? Do I have something to contribute to group discussion so that my group members will think that I am a smart student? What if I have something in mind but cannot get my meaning across? How am I going to criticize my team members' papers without offending them? Do I have the knowledge and expertise to critique my peers' papers? Will I be able to benefit from the comments made by my group members?

Having such questions is very normal among students who have never done peer response activities before or students who have had limited experience with peer response. While these questions could be indications of shyness, insecurity, anxiety, and feelings of inadequacy—often associated with students with little or no prior successful experience with peer response—an adequate amount of time given to allowing students to get to know one another before any serious peer response work starts will go a long way toward easing and comforting them. Some warm-up activities—such as allowing students to introduce themselves, do some short activities together, make and wear name tags, tell a story about a funny thing that happened recently, or interview a classmate in class—can be designed to enable students to get to know each other, to feel comfortable, and to feel a sense of belonging.

## Group Norms and Conformity

Group norms refer to the development of certain patterns and behavior while establishing goals and agendas during the initial stages of group formation. A group needs to be able to establish patterns that it feels comfortable with, and this pattern also needs to be visible. For instance, in order to respect group members, each individual student in a peer response group has to read other group members' papers before peer response activities. Oftentimes, we find some students sitting in a circle busy reading the papers being critiqued and coming up with questions that are either superficial or inappropriate because they did not read the paper carefully earlier. This will seriously debilitate group dynamics and will have some repercussions on group cohesion. Some group members may show up on time but without the peer response sheets or the paper under discussion. Their carelessness may be annoying to other group members, since the reciprocal relationship among group members will be harmed if there is an imbalance in receiving and giving feedback. Thus, certain rules or norms within a group should be negotiated from early on, and once they are formed, every group member should try hard to act accordingly. This is very important in sustaining group work.

Rules or norms to be negotiated among group members in

peer response should include but not be limited to the following.

- How long should the peer response activity last?
- What major areas (e.g., content, organization, grammar, mechanics) should the comments focus on?
- What is the order of commenting and turn-taking?
- Who should communicate with a person who is absent?
- Is a person who is absent for a peer response activity responsible for giving written comments to peers ahead of time and/or immediately afterward?
- What actions should a group take regarding excessive absence and lack of preparation of individual group members? (E.g., Should a person be excluded from the group after a certain number of times?)
- Should drafts revised as the result of peer response be circulated among group members?
- Should a reflection section be built into each peer response activity to allow group members to share their experiences and make suggestions for improvement?

Having students negotiate these rules will enable them to feel more secure and engaged in the peer response task. However, these rules should not be seen as inflexible—as the groups members become more familiar with the response tasks and with each other, it may be necessary to revise the rules and/or add or delete certain components. Different tasks may also necessitate different rules. Therefore, the initial rules can be viewed as a starting point that can be changed across time and tasks.

### Task Achievement and Group Maintenance

Completing peer response tasks (responding and critiquing group members' papers and convincing group members to revise papers based on peer comments) and maintaining effective working relationships among group members are interconnected. Good group dynamics can usually enable a group to complete tasks in a timely and effective fashion. On the other hand, effective completion of tasks reflects the collaborative efforts of a group. The quality of the group experience can be enhanced if group members are aware of the significance of both the task and the maintenance aspects of group dynamics. The quality and effectiveness of the group will be improved when all members make a contribution to the way the group works, as well as to the tasks that the group is undertaking.

In order to maintain group cohesion and dynamics, active participation in peer response activities is very important. It requires giving recognition, demonstrating acceptance and openness, and being friendly and responsive to all members. Those with a capacity to work toward creating greater harmony and consensus can play an important role in maintaining the work of groups. As we know, some group members who are task-oriented might do most of the talking in peer response activities. Such people focus only on completing the task and sometimes become preoccupied with the task without concern for giving other group members opportunities to contribute to the discussion; this might produce negative feelings and resentment among other group members. A group needs to be kept on track with regard to tasks, but when maintenance of intergroup relations is ignored, the group's effectiveness is at risk.

In peer response activities, tension might also arise if comments with good intentions are not phrased in a socioculturally appropriate way or if communication breaks down when the speaker's comments are misunderstood by the listener. Therefore, peer response activities in L2 writing sometimes involve more than giving or receiving comments from peers. Peer response might be considered as a good opportunity for negotiating meaning and communicating about real tasks.

## Setting Goals and Developing Agendas

While a personal or individual goal is one that is held by one member of a group, the goal of a group is ideally held by enough members that the group can be said to be working toward its achievement. All groups have goals, and every person who joins a group brings his or her own personal goals. Goals for peer response activities can be specified by giving feedback or comments on each paper written by group members, by interactive negotiation of meaning between the author and other group members, and by receiving or rejecting the comments made by group members. Some of the issues that may need to be negotiated include rules for turn-taking, the roles of the participants, and practical concerns about absence and/or lack of preparation on peer response day. For instance, what happens if one person has not read the group members' papers and therefore has not completed the peer response sheets that are essential for face-to-face peer response activities? Or what happens if a group member forgets to bring the paper and/or completed peer response sheets on the peer response day? These situations occur frequently, and rules should specify the consequences of this behavior and the remedial procedures that may follow it.

Establishing the group goal is an essential first step in establishing an effective peer response work environment. In the process of establishing a common goal and a common agenda, group members need to be open-minded and demonstrate a spirit of generosity and acceptance of each other's points of view and contributions. Because this is an early task in terms of the group's development, group members need to work together to listen to each other's ideas and contributions. Sometimes, issues of power and authority, in terms of who should be the group leader or who should facilitate the peer response activities, tend to surface during this process. One strategy L2 writing teachers can use is to make sure that group leadership is negotiated rather than assigned and ask students to rotate the leadership position each time they engage in peer response activities; both of these guidelines could be specified in the goals. In this way, everyone in a group can have opportunities to contribute to the group discussion and assume the responsibilities of a peer, as well as a group leader.

## Coping with Group Conflicts

During peer response activities, there are some occasions when group members do not get along or have opinions that are so different that personal friction and conflicts occur. Sometimes there are issues of trust that arise regarding peer comments, especially concerning some rhetorical issues, as members of the same group are usually at the same level as far as writing skills are concerned. Some group members might withdraw from making comments or simply ignore the suggestions made by peers. For instance, in a recent study on the effects of peer versus teacher comments on student revisions, some peers' comments on organization or rhetorical devices were only taken into consideration when the teacher made the same comments (Liu and Sadler 2000). Some group members might also feel threatened when those who are very critical of peers' papers are the ones whose own writing is full of mistakes.

There is sometimes a lack of trust among peers, especially when they are from different disciplines (Liu 1998). This potential conflict, if not well resolved, could lead to a climate of lack of trust or acceptance and could cause some group members to close off or withdraw from the group. It is very helpful to encourage all group members to participate and to encourage each other to participate at all times in peer response activities. As personal frictions can emerge among group members at any time during group activities, strong feelings of "ownership" and a sense of belonging can become very important to some group members. Group members should value themselves and what they know and be prepared to assist other group members and share what they know. They should ask questions, speak out about matters that they consider important, and be open to new ideas or different opinions.

There are a number of strategies the teacher can use to help resolve group conflicts in peer response activities. First of all, the teacher should try to investigate the sources of conflicts by careful observation, talking with people who report the conflicts, as well as with those who are reported to be causing the conflicts. Sometimes if the teacher acts on a conflict too quickly, without having different perspectives from the different people involved, the results will be negative. Second, the teacher should provide resources and concrete examples or evidence to help students resolve conflicts. For instance, if the author and the group members do not agree with one another, the teacher could, rather than taking a side, show them some examples from a book or from some other resource or act as the facilitator in negotiating meaning, reminding group members that the author still makes the final decision. Third, if personal conflicts occur, the teacher should determine whether there is a need to pull out a student who is under severe criticism by his or her group members and place this student into another group to tone down the conflicts. Last but not least, the teacher should try to act in the group as a participant and offer on-the-spot advice and suggestions for the group.

In summary, once peer response groups are formed, sensitivity and responsibility should coexist in order to sustain quality group work. When students get along in a group, they tend to feel secure and make greater efforts to change the things that make people uncomfortable or slow down the group activity. A sense of cohesiveness or group identity can develop. With time, group members may tend to become more open with each other, although sometimes, because of personalities or diverse cultural backgrounds, students in a group might not be able to achieve harmony and efficiency at the same time. A good, cohesive group is one in which responsibility is shared; such a group is better organized and more efficient. These conditions can provide a good working climate for peer response groups. Group cohesion, to a great extent, relies on the interpersonal communication skills of group members.

As teachers who facilitate students' peer response activities, we should be sensitive to a number of issues. How are members expressing themselves? Does everyone in a group get a chance to talk? Are students able to express what they have in mind? How well do students listen to each other? How do members respond to each other? Are they critical of and/or receptive to each other's ideas, or do they ignore some students' comments? Is the group moving toward achieving its purpose? Are there any power struggles in assuming the role of leader in a group? What is the climate of the group? How clearly are the goals understood and accepted? To make a group work, there must be some interaction (physical, verbal, nonverbal, emotional, etc.) among group members who are sensitive to the existence of the group and aware of the needs of individual members within the group. Of course, group members must share some purpose or goal in being together and be committed to the group.

## Suggestions for Teachers

Based on the discussion in this chapter, we have the following suggestions for writing teachers who are considering options for grouping conducive to the effectiveness of peer response activities in the writing classroom.

- Getting students acquainted through interaction is the first step toward successful peer response activities. It is advisable to give students adequate time to familiarize themselves with one another. For instance, students can play a game called "Who's who?" by asking as many classmates as possible the same set of questions within a certain amount of time and finding out some common characteristics these classmates share. Having students pair up to interview and introduce each other allows them to get as much information as possible from a peer and then introduce that peer to the class. There are many ways to engage students in getting to know their peers. Sometimes the instructor can use some mini–peer response activities, such as the discussion of one question in groups, to give students opportunities to understand what peer response means to them as group members, what their responsibilities are in a group, what goals and objectives they can negotiate with their peers, and how they can communicate effectively in peer response groups. Having such preliminary experiences with peer response is vital in helping students make informed decisions in grouping.

- Teachers should be aware of different options in forming groups and the potential benefits and problems with each formation. There are basically four commonly practiced grouping options: self-initiated grouping (students form groups based on their own needs or convenience); assigned grouping (students are placed into groups by the teacher randomly or purposefully); task-based grouping (switching students among groups across assignments); and long-standing grouping (stabilizing groups throughout the semester). Each of these options can work well under certain circumstances or not work well, and each can affect group dynamics and chemistry positively or negatively. The teacher should explain to the students in training the pros and cons of each of these options, give students opportunities to try different options, and invite them to reflect on their experiences with these grouping options and to offer suggestions as to what they prefer and what might work better for them.

- Whenever possible, the teacher should establish communication channels for feedback (e.g., E-mail, listservs) to allow individual students to talk with the teacher about any concerns regarding the group work that might be inappropriate for students to discuss in groups. The teacher should also periodically assess the effects of peer response among groups and make necessary adjustments for grouping across tasks to maximize input and hone students' communication and writing skills for a variety of readers/audiences.

- While considering grouping options, the instructor should keep in mind that the number of students in a group could affect the effectiveness of the grouping. Although there is no magic number for a group, the instructor should make decisions based on the total number of students in a given class. For instance, it is perhaps wise for the instructor to avoid assigning more than five students to long-standing groups unless these students know one another well and are willing to participate. It is always good to start with small groups, since they come to agreement and finish tasks more efficiently and can easily be regrouped if necessary. If there are about 12 to 16 students in a class, groups of three are ideal. But if a class consists of more than 30 students, having 10 groups of three is not manageable because of physical space restrictions and noise factors. In this case, a group of five or six would be ideal.

- Each and every student should realize the potential of being an active participant in collaboration. As will be discussed in the following chapter, students who participate in peer response activities often play different roles. Some are more active than others are, and some are good at face-to-face communication, while others are better at communicating their ideas through writing. The teacher might need to consider a number of factors that directly or indirectly influence the effects of peer response activities. These factors include: group size (pairs/dyads to groups of more than six); gender and age (e.g., bigger groups with more experienced responders, smaller with beginners); cultural backgrounds, beliefs, and communication rituals; areas of study; the nature of the peer response task; the length of group work and attention span; proficiency in writing and other language skills; the total number of students in a class; and the time given to peer response activities. The teacher should consider which options are more conducive to peer learning at particular points in time in peer response grouping development. For instance, matching students with different linguistic and cultural backgrounds might sometimes be more appropriate than matching students according to their areas of study. Likewise, matching students according to the topics/themes of their writing might occasionally be more appropriate than matching students based on their diverse backgrounds in order to allow feedback from a general audience. In one way or another, the teacher should always allow students with good reasons to switch into different groups.

- While mixing students with different linguistic abilities, cultural backgrounds, cognitive styles (e.g., field-dependent vs. field-independent), and communication patterns (e.g., total integration, conditional interaction, marginal participation, and silent observation, per Liu 2001) can be effective in fostering a supportive peer environment, attention should be given to the fact that some learners (those who are or who consider themselves to be at more advanced writing levels than their peers) might not have a sense of achievement and satisfaction, since their output exceeds their input. That is, more advanced writers might prefer to be in a group where they can find intellectual stimulation and challenge from peers at the same proficiency level or in the same major. On these occasions, different demands might be made of different students, and more challenging tasks and expectations might be given to those who feel the need to be challenged.

- As the discussion of homogeneous versus heterogeneous groups implies, there are virtually no genuinely homogeneous groups in L2 writing classrooms in either ESL or EFL settings. Though the nature of heterogeneity might be different, the L2 writing teacher should embrace the diversity and educate students to work with peers who are different from them in many aspects in order to foster a healthy intercultural communication environment.

- Students should set the ground rules for peer response, either as a group or as a whole class, and agree to follow these rules. The rules may need to take into account such issues as roles, modes, turn-taking, and practical concerns such as absence and/or lack of preparation for peer response.

- The teacher should be sensitive to the dynamics and chemistry of groups. Whenever there is a conflict or potential conflict, the teacher should try to investigate the nature and the source of the conflict and find solutions to resolve it. These solutions include talking with individual group members, providing examples and resources, removing a student from a group, and participating in the group discussion.

# Chapter 4
## Modes and Roles in Peer Response

Peer response activities take place in different modes, and the different modes affect the roles participants play. Peer response modes refer to formats—written, oral, or a combination of both. The recent developments of computer-assisted language learning (CALL) and computer-mediated communication (CMC) have added new dimensions to modes. For instance, what is traditionally considered to be oral peer response can take the form of synchronous communication through on-line discussion, with all the peers participating in the activity at the same time. Likewise, written peer response can be ongoing, through E-mail or listservs that offer the opportunity for asynchronous comments, with all the participants arranging their own time to communicate with peers. In terms of the roles of the participants in peer response, students will sometimes be the recipients of response, when their papers are being discussed, and sometimes be the critics, when they offer their comments on the paper being discussed and make suggestions for changes. Moreover, two-way negotiation of meaning always exists between the author of the paper and the peers who make comments. The instructor's role may also vary. Sometimes the instructor will be a nonparticipating observer, making sure that everything is going smoothly and offering ready help whenever necessary. At other times, the instructor might participate in peer response activities, doing whatever is required as a peer. This chapter will discuss these issues crucial to the success of peer response activities.

## Modes of Peer Response

Modes in peer response refer to different peer response formats. We can roughly divide peer response modes into two types: the *traditional* mode and the *innovative* mode. While the former includes both written response through pen and paper and face-to-face communication (i.e., peers sitting together and making comments on each other's papers), the latter relies heavily on CMC, which breaks the traditional boundaries of written and oral formats. These different modes will be discussed.

### Traditional Modes

The written format of peer response is the most common. When students read their peers' drafts, they are reading with a number of guiding questions from the peer response sheet, such as: "What is the thesis statement of the paper?" "Is the paper well organized?" "What are the main strengths and weaknesses of the paper?" "What part of this essay do you like most and why?" Searching for the answers to these questions while reading drafts written by peers will make peer response more focused and engaging. Written feedback in the traditional mode makes it easy for students to make marginal notes and comments and sometimes draw a line between words or sentences, underline or circle some phrases for attention, and even use colored pens to denote different types of comments. It is convenient for students to read and comment on papers without space and time limitations. Often students use written comments to assist face-to-face communication. Due to the time restrictions on peer response activities in class, sometimes every student in a group does not have the opportunity to make extensive comments on all peers' papers. With detailed written comments, students can highlight salient points that they wish to comment on in oral peer response activities, thus allowing equal time for other students in a group.

Of course, traditional written comments are not without constraints. Students often complain about poor handwriting and a lack of consistency in making comments. That is, some students might comment in such a way that the author does not read and understand the comments as originally intended. Moreover, it is often difficult to change the comments once they are made. Additionally, sometimes the handwriting of a peer is too obvious, when anonymity is preferred, because the obvious recognition of handwriting will make the acceptance or rejection of certain comments very subjective.

To resolve these potential drawbacks of written peer response, the writing teacher often prefers to have an oral peer response session as a continuation of the written session. In this way, students are given opportunities to clarify queries, to negotiate meanings, and to probe further what is going on in the minds of the author and those who have made comments. Oral peer response also provides opportunities for students to improve their communicative competence and to get to know each other better as peers. However, oral peer response activities could marginalize students who might not communicate with competence or who might be uncomfortable expressing their ideas openly and criticizing their peers' papers. As a result, comments may be general and superficial, which is not helpful to authors who are looking for more specific suggestions and hoping to understand why certain suggestions have been made.

While the success of oral response in a group often relies on prior written comments (e.g., students have written down their comments on a peer response sheet, either structured or open-ended, or have made marginal comments on the drafts written by their peers), the effectiveness of written comments also depends on oral communication and negotiation. The combination of both oral and written modes in peer response seems to be practical and beneficial.

With the advancement of computer technology, traditional peer response formats have taken on a new dimension. In an oral peer response format, for instance, students can comment instantly and simultaneously through computers, as if they were talking on the spot; this is often referred to as synchronous response and is exemplified by MOO interaction or chatroom discussion. Likewise, in written peer response formats, students can also use computer-mediated (asynchronous) response by posting their comments through E-mail or a listserv and engaging in ongoing dialogues. Computer-based—or innovative—modes of peer response are discussed next.

### Computer-Mediated Modes

Computer-mediated peer response refers to both asynchronous communication, such as E-mail, and to virtual synchronous conversation in multi-user domains object-oriented (MOOs—on-line chat rooms that allow users to hold virtual real-time conversations with other users connected to the same MOO via the Internet). Such computer-mediated communication—exchanges of textual, audio, and video information through computer networks—can afford an additional means of learner-to-learner communication, one that is possibly less anxiety-provoking than face-to-face interaction. In addition, CMC extends the interaction possibilities beyond the classroom walls and hence "beyond its time constraints and the usual limited circle of interlocutors of classroom pair and group work" (Belcher 1999, 255). This aspect of convenience is often cited as being an important advantage of MOOs for classroom communication, as it enables participants to collaborate outside of the classroom on their own time (Egbert, Chao, and Hanson-Smith 1999). Research in second language classrooms indicates that networked computers do indeed enhance opportunities and motivation for authentic interaction and negotiation of meaning (Kern 1995); reduce anxiety and produce more talk (Fanderclai 1995; Kelm 1992); and improve linguistic proficiency and increase self-confidence (Beauvois and Eledge 1996).

In ESL/EFL writing classes, observations of using CMC in various formats also indicate students' enhanced confidence in writing and increased quantity in both peer and teacher feedback (Braine 1997). Researchers (Rheingold 1993; Sproull and Kiesler 1991) also suggest that CMC has great potential for leveling the playing field in the multilinguistic, multicultural classroom, thus empowering minority students or non–native English speaking students in composition classrooms with linguistically and culturally diverse backgrounds (Belcher 1999). As oral classroom participation is not encouraged in many countries where attentive listening and students' silence are expected (Liu 2000), peer response via CMC seems greatly facilitated by synchronized interaction. Warschauer (1996) found much more equitable conversations in the CMC mode than in face-to-face contact because the less vocal students seemed to participate more. This finding was confirmed by Sullivan and Pratt (1996), whose study showed full student participation in electronic discourse as compared to 50 percent participation in face-to-face interaction. In terms of the quality of interaction, Warschauer (1996) reports that the participants in his study tended to express their own ideas during electronic communication rather than directly answering questions posed to them, suggesting increased creativity. Also, the electronic discussions involved significantly more complex sentence structures than face-to-face discussions did.

It seems obvious that research in this area has already observed and identified both quantitative and qualitative differences between electronic interactions and face-to-face interactions in peer response activities. But several questions remain. Does the use of a technology-enhanced synchronous interaction mode (a MOO) versus a traditional synchronous interaction mode (face-to-face communication) result in a differential distribution of peer comments according to area (global vs. local); type of comments (evaluation, clarification, suggestion, alteration); and the nature of each type of comment (revision oriented vs. non–revision oriented)? To what extent do students revise their papers based on peer comments made in traditional versus technology-enhanced commenting and interaction modes?

To address these issues, Liu and Sadler (2000) conducted classroom research investigating whether different commenting and interaction modes (technology-enhanced vs. traditional) make a difference in the *area* (global vs. local), the *type* (evaluation, clarification, suggestion, alteration), and the *nature* (revision oriented vs. non–revision oriented) of comments by both peers and the teacher and how the observed differences affected students' revisions. Their findings show that the overall number of comments, the percentage of revision oriented comments, and consequently the overall number of revisions made by the technology-enhanced group were greater than those made by the traditional group. This study suggests that the use of an electronic peer response mode may serve as an effective tool for the revision process.

Nevertheless, several problems remain with regard to the use of technology-enhanced peer response. First of all, students might prefer certain formats to others, regardless of the benefits to revision. The results of Liu and Sadler's (2000) study indicate that although the students in the technology-enhanced group enjoyed using the MOO interaction feature, they disliked the Microsoft Word commenting feature. The students, in general, considered their experience using the MOO to be "fun." This seemed to result in a greater level of comfort for them with this method of communication. In addition, the lack of face-to-face interaction seemed to be beneficial to some students whose cultural backgrounds do not encourage such interaction in a classroom environment (Liu 2000). In other words, a discrepancy existed between the benefits students in the technology-enhanced group received from peer response and their dislike for using certain features such as Microsoft Word commenting features as the changes made are not revealed at the first glance.

According to Liu and Sadler (2000), students using the computer-assisted commenting feature tended to focus more on the electronic drafts of peers' essays, while students using a traditional written format tended to be more dependent on the peer response sheet. This pattern is important, since students who replied on the peer response sheet were not likely to make comments that went beyond the scope of that sheet. Students who used technology-enhanced peer response, on the other hand, may have begun by answering the questions from the sheet, which usually serves as a guideline for students' comments, but then they may have gone beyond that sheet and made further comments on their peers' papers. The stronger connection to the text might give students more flexibility in offering comments to their peers by allowing them to integrate not only the questions from the peer response sheet but also their own thoughts regarding the text they are responding to.

While using technology-enhanced commenting modes in peer response is beneficial, there is always a concern with the time necessary to familiarize students with software or get them settled using computers. This problem can be aggravated when a class period is short or when students only use computer-equipped classrooms once or twice a week. In addition, the amount of work required for students to comment on their peers' papers via computer is usually very extensive. This is partially because of the procedures necessary in getting started (e.g., inserting the disc, finding the correct files on the disc, waiting for a virus scan, opening Microsoft Word, opening the insert/comment feature, etc.). In addition, once the students get started, they have to follow certain steps in making their comments (e.g., highlighting the desired text, clicking on the insert/comment button, clicking on the insert/comment text field, and typing the comment). With traditional commenting, on the other hand, only the last step is needed. In other words, students can write down their comments without going through all these technical procedures.

Another problem of electronic peer response is the need for computer access. Students must have access to computers in order to respond electronically. On the other hand, traditional peer response only requires a pen or pencil and may be done anywhere. Furthermore, the traditional written format tends to encourage responders to focus more on global issues in the draft.

Electronic peer response can be assisted by computer software. One commonly used type of software is called CommonSpace. An important feature of CommonSpace is that multiple columns can be created so that comments can be linked to specific portions of the writer's text. When the comment is clicked on, the relevant portion of the text is highlighted. To investigate whether there are differences in text processing and, if so, how they affect the extent to which students provide comments on peers' papers, Bloch and Brutt-Griffler (2001) compared a traditional method (the pen-and-paper hard-copy method) and the on-line method (using CommonSpace) in their postadmission ESL classes at a Midwestern U.S. university. The study revealed that pen-and-paper comments were harder to read, while CommonSpace comments were easier to find and read. While the paper-and-pen comments tended to be general in nature, the Common-Space comments were usually much more detailed. A further finding, through discourse analysis of students' peer responses in both traditional mode and on-line mode, indicates that when students responded on the computer screen using the features of CommonSpace, they tended to comment before reading the full draft; however, when using a hard copy of the text, they were inclined to read the entire essay before making any comments. The results show a consistent difference in the kind of feedback students provided to each other using the two different commenting modes. While students using CommonSpace tended to focus more on grammatical and sentence-level concerns than rhetorical concerns, students using the traditional method tended to concentrate more on global issues such as general impressions, content, and rhetoric.

In summary, modes of peer response are multiple, and each mode has its own advantages and disadvantages in various contexts. While computer-enhanced peer response modes—such as Microsoft Word's editing features, MOOs, and CommonSpace—are exciting, innovative, and worth exploring, the functions of the traditional written and oral modes are still valuable and essential, especially for instructors who have not overcome the anxiety of using modern technology in their teaching or for whom computer resources have not been adequately provided or sufficient time for training students to use software has not been built into the syllabus design. Nevertheless, more studies are needed to provide evidence of the pros and cons of each peer response mode, of what different modes can be combined to produce positive effects on peer response, and of how these varied modes can be implemented in classrooms.

Each mode of peer response—whether traditional (written, oral, or written plus oral) or computer-mediated—has benefits and constraints that the teacher will need to weigh depending on the skill level (especially with regard to computers) and interests of students. The benefits and constraints of utilizing different peer response modes are outlined in table 6.

**TABLE 6.   Benefits and Constraints of Different Peer Response Modes**

| Modes | Pros | Cons |
| --- | --- | --- |
| Traditional | | |
| Written | Provides guided questions for response | Hard to read sometimes due to poor handwriting |
| | Provides opportunities for marginal comments and graphic linkages | Difficult to change once comments are made on paper |
| | Encourages both global and local comments | Space to insert marginal comments lacking |
| | Serves as basis for oral comments | Anonymity sometimes questionable |
| | Facilitates face-to-face communication | |
| Oral | Allows negotiation of meaning | Highly dependent on individuals' communication skills |
| | Provides opportunities for clarification, probing, and in-depth discussion in nonlinear fashion | Silence those from cultures that discourage open communication |
| | Enhances communicative competence | Comments may be general and superficial |
| | Connects people's thoughts for both speakers and listeners | |
| | Benefits the whole group in action | |

*(continued)*

**TABLE 6—*Continued***

| Modes | Pros | Cons |
|---|---|---|
| Innovative | | |
| Synchronous | Provides platform for discussion without students necessarily being together<br>Highly engaging and stimulating<br>Encourages playful atmosphere and improvisation<br>Enhances motivation and group cohesion | Dependent on typing speed<br>Turn-taking problematic<br>Short on completion of meaning under time pressure<br>Uncertainty for the author receiving multiple and perhaps controversial comments simultaneously<br>Chaotic if prior responding arrangements are not well made<br>Encourages more "impression" comments than specific text-related comments |
| Asynchronous | Caters to individual needs and learning styles<br>Allows sufficient time for students to compose their comments<br>Allows space and time for more thoughtful comments and responses<br>Good writing practice in itself<br>Accumulates messages for retrieval and response<br>Allows both group and individual interaction | Time-consuming<br>Inconvenient if computer facilities at home and/or on campus are lacking<br>Uncertainty and anxiety caused by indefinite wait for responses |

## Roles in Peer Response

In peer response activities, the roles of the participants are multiple. In any group work, there must be a leader who serves in the role of facilitator to get the ball rolling, to maintain the time flow, and to reconcile disputes. Such a leadership role should be rotated among the group members so that everyone in a group can have the experience of being the leader. This increases the awareness of each group member and thus makes each a better participant. Apart from playing the leadership role, each student should also be a good listener, one who is willing to listen to others' critiques and comments rather than dominating the discussion without giving others opportunities to voice their opinions and make comments. Taking an active role in discussion and collaborating with peers is essential for the success of peer response. When the paper of a team member is being critiqued, the author of the paper should be open-minded, willing to listen to both positive and negative comments and to take the opportunity to probe and negotiate meaning in order to understand why certain comments are made.

The teacher, too, can play different roles in peer response activities. One important role for the teacher is that of a facilitator who supervises group formation and peer response instruction. The teacher is sometimes a monitor who oversees the processes of peer response, addressing issues arising from peer response activities and serving as a timekeeper to make sure that students spend equal amounts of time on each other's papers. Moreover, the teacher sometimes can participate in peer response activities as a participant-observer, contributing to discussion as a member of the team and confirming uncertainties and answering questions whenever appropriate.

### How do students participate in peer response activities?

Students' participation in peer response activities can be characterized by several patterns. Some students are active participants, who not only prepare well ahead of time but also are fully engaged in contributing to group discussions. Some might be cautious, offering only those comments they have prepared beforehand but not engaging in further clarification and probing. Others might be very passive, sitting there as if they are not present, partly because of their shy nature and partly because of their lack of preparation.

#### Active Participants

Active participants in peer response activities characteristically mingle well with the flow of the class, knowing exactly when to speak up, what to address, and how. Their participation is not only a reflection of their thorough preparation but also of their ability to make spontaneous comments and negotiate meanings. Active participants are usually aware of the appropriate role a student should play in a group and of what a student should do to contribute to the success of group work. Liu (1996) noticed that many ESL students who were very quiet in his composition class reversed their roles once they were in groups, becoming active speakers instead of attentive listeners. This role reversal is largely related to students' educational and cultural backgrounds, coupled with a number of other factors. For example, do students have something to contribute to the group discussion? If students have not read the drafts written by their group members, how can they be expected to make substantial comments? On the other hand, if a student has read the papers well before coming to the peer response session, whether this student will be an active participant in discussion is still unpredictable, as he or she might not have found much to comment on. Likewise, if a student does have something to say yet has concerns about speaking in English, this student will likely end up remaining silent most of the time in peer response activities.

### Somewhat Active Participants

As is discussed earlier, students' participation in peer response is constrained by a number of factors—sociocultural, cognitive, affective, linguistic, or environmental. Students might have a high level of motivation to participate in group discussion, but their actual participation and interaction with their peers in a group are limited. These students are still figuring out when to speak up in class, what to address, and how. Their own social identities and their perceptions of what is appropriate behavior in a group in their home cultures often serve as reminders before they take chances to speak up. They might carefully monitor their behavior before each attempt and slowly but surely nudge their way into the discovery of their comfort zone in group participation. These students' participation is peripheral and is usually compensated for by attentive listening and note-taking, as well as by discussion in informal homogeneous groups (i.e., groups formed from the same linguistic and cultural backgrounds) after class. These students are less adventurous and usually rely on the familiar communication strategies of their home cultures to cope with what the target culture requires. When they occasionally speak up in groups, they are often poised and confident in what they say because each turn-taking is usually the result of careful thinking and internal rehearsal to avoid grammatical mistakes. Through self-monitoring and trial and error, students' confidence level is increased by the reward of their meaningful suggestions being accepted by their peers.

### Inactive Participants

Inactive participants in peer response groups are those who either withdraw from verbal/vocal participation in group discussion or who seemingly agree with but do not elaborate on comments or suggestions by other group members. These students tend to rely on nonverbal communication strategies to show agreement or disagreement with peers. The multiple factors underlying their silence in peer response activities are extremely complicated and often cause misinterpretation and misunderstanding. Having more than one student of this type in a group sometimes can have a negative impact on group dynamics and chemistry. For example, active participants might feel taken advantage of because their contributions are not returned with enthusiasm or their papers do not receive the same degree of commenting.

These peer response participation patterns can be placed on a continuum from the most active to the least active. However, some individual students' identifications with the least active or most active participation patterns are not static. As the result of their changing perceptions of peer response activities and the interaction of multiple factors—such as increased or decreased self-confidence or instantaneous positive or negative experiences of a communication event—

students can be expected to bounce back and forth along the continuum as their experience with peer response accumulates. Revealed within each peer response participation pattern are some shared characteristics and some marked differences in students' perceptions of peer response activities, as affected by multiple factors.

To encourage students to be active participants in peer response activities, the teacher should allow students sufficient time to read their peers' papers and provide concrete guidelines for responding. For instance, depending on the writing task and the purpose of peer response, the peer response sheet should be constructed and presented in class with examples before being used for a real purpose. The teacher should also be sensitive to the linguistic and cultural backgrounds of the students and encourage those who are not used to verbal communication, in terms of offering open criticism or handling disagreement, to speak their minds without having too many concerns. Moreover, students should learn turn-taking strategies in order to feel comfortable in participating in discussions actively.

### What is the role of a facilitator?

One of the factors contributing to the success of any peer response group activity is having a good facilitator. A facilitator is someone in a group who takes the leadership role during a peer response activity. This role can be rotated among group members. No matter who assumes the role, the facilitator must ensure that the peer response is conducted as smoothly as possible and in ways that are consistent with the learning goals of the group. For a facilitator, certain responsibilities are associated with each stage of peer response—before peer response, during peer response, and after peer response—as outlined in table 7.

It is extremely important for any peer response group in L2 writing classrooms to establish a set of boundaries for the group facilitator at the beginning. It should not be assumed that the group facilitator will play a central role in the group.

**TABLE 7.   Responsibilities of Peer Response Facilitator**

| Before Peer Response | During Peer Response | After Peer Response |
|---|---|---|
| Know your role as a facilitator in addition to your role as a peer. | Establish an agreement and objectives for the group. Make sure that everyone in the group is ready before the peer response activity starts. | Give enough time for peers to reflect on their experiences and make suggestions for improving the peer response process next time. |
| Make sure that everyone in a group has copies of peers' papers and has read them ahead of time. | Make it clear to everyone how much time is allocated for the peer response activity as a whole and approximately how many minutes should be spent on each paper. | Take notes, make suggestions, and discuss the feasibility of incorporating the suggestions in the next peer response activity. |
| Make sure that everyone in the group has completed the peer response sheet to guide their comments and questions. | Make known to everyone in the group the sequence of the peer response in terms of whose paper is being critiqued first, second, etc. | Consult and communicate with the teacher about concerns and issues of the peer response group. |
| Make sure the physical environment is properly set up—chairs in the right places, appropriate heating and lighting, and a location that is not too noisy. | If the group is unsure of what needs to be done next, suggest that the group take time out for discussion, in an effort to achieve some consensus before proceeding. | Reflect on your own experience as facilitator and know exactly what you need to improve on for the next time. |

Like any other member of the group, the group facilitator may contribute ideas and suggestions for action or volunteer to do things. It is important for the group facilitator to establish a democratic and equal partnership with the members of the group in terms of power and skills and try to act as a consultant rather than as an authoritative supervisor or leader.

### What is the role of the author in peer response?

One of the characteristics of peer response activities is that each group member's paper is critiqued in turn. That is, each student will serve as the recipient of comments from group members. It is sometimes easier to make comments than to receive comments, especially when these comments are harsh, controversial, or off target. Therefore, while making appropriate comments in peer response activities is essential, being aware of the strategies and skills necessary in receiving comments is equally important for the success of peer response activities. The student whose paper is being commented on is usually in a vulnerable position, which requires courage on the part of the author—courage to be challenged and courage to challenge the challenge. As comments are made in different areas, such as rhetoric, organization, mechanics, and grammar, the writer should be able to judge the worth of comments, to show agreement or disagreement, to clarify what was originally in mind, and to negotiate meaning. Sometimes, the comments themselves are valuable, but the *way* that these comments are made might not be appropriate. For instance, a command rather than a suggestion—"You should change this paragraph!" instead of "Could you please make this paragraph clearer?"—might sound very offensive to the writer. But the writer should be able to clarify the intention behind the comment and find a way to negotiate the meaning—"Does this paragraph bother you? How do you think I should change it to make it clearer?"

One of the observations language teachers often make is that students in a group tend to be very agreeable to whatever peers have to say. In this way, the interaction becomes one-way only, and the writer of the paper tends to become a passive acceptor and make corrections without questioning why. Part of the reason for this is that these students care too much about their image in a group; they mistakenly believe that their agreement with whatever comments are made by their peers will foster group dynamics and harmony. This is especially true among Asian students, who consider group cohesion more important than personal opinions when there is a conflict. As one ESL student from Japan confessed in an intermediate ESL composition class at a Midwestern U.S. university (personal communication, 7 May 1996):

As all my group members are my friends and we get along with each other very well, I think they are very polite in making comments on my paper. I do not want to argue with them, and I try to change my paper according to their opinions even though I know some of their comments are not right. You know, I do not want them to think that I am not listening to them. Yes, I will always reread my paper and sometimes if I do have different opinions than my friends, I will add a note in the paper to ask the teacher. It is just so hard to deny my friends, and I feel much better in a group that everyone is nice and kind.

On the other hand, sometimes a student writer might reverse this role and become very resistant to peers' comments. Such a student would tend to disagree with whatever his or her group members had to say about a paper. Either being very argumentative or simply refusing to make changes, a student could become very emotional, regarding comments as personal attacks and thus making everyone in a group uncomfortable. Obviously, in this case the teacher should make a decision to pull the student out of the group and to discover the sources of conflicts. One possible solution would be to utilize the peer response sheet on which written comments from peers are offered. Another possible solution would be for the teacher to talk with the student and point out the value of peer comments, using some concrete examples.

### What should the role of the teacher be in peer response?

In most cases, once the students are divided into groups, the teacher's role is that of a facilitator or a "troubleshooter," making sure that everything is moving smoothly and serving as a resource for questions or disputes. Constantly moving from one group to another will indicate the teacher's presence and awareness of group activities. However, instead of being a nonparticipating observer, the teacher can actually participate in a group and contribute to the discussion by playing the role of a group member. Although having the teacher present could affect how group members react and respond in group activities, if the teacher makes an effort to read students' papers carefully and complete the peer response sheets as everyone else in a group does, then the teacher's role will be closer to that of a peer and his or her comments will be considered as a peer's. In fact, in an effort to participate in peer response activities as a peer in his ESL composition classes, Liu (1996) noticed an increased level of participation from all the students and an increased number of comments made by the students.

Although an instructor's image will probably not be altered in the students' minds, it is possible for an instructor to shorten the distance between her or himself and her or his students by doing what a student is required to do for peer response activities. The instructor, for instance, can read a student's paper and complete the peer response sheet. The instructor can also participate in peer response activities as a peer. For instance, instead of assuming the role of an authoritative figure by giving assertive comments, the instructor can ask more probing questions to allow the students to try to come up with solutions themselves. The instructor should also be careful not to give comments before students have an opportunity. It can be argued that the teacher can never be a peer, but an instructor's willingness to assume the role of a peer can bring not only rapport with but also respect from students.

## Suggestions for Teachers

- As is discussed in this chapter, peer response is more effective if different modes (written, oral, written plus oral, computer-mediated) are incorporated. While choosing various modes in peer response, the instructor has to consider the interconnections between and among the modes and arrange their use in a logical and time-efficient way. For instance, sufficient time should be allowed for students to read their peers' papers before they are invited to give comments. It is always helpful to provide a few guiding questions for peer response. These questions may be open-ended, allowing students to focus on some general issues, such as the thesis statement, the overall organization of the paper, the major grammatical mistakes, and the transitions in the paper. Sometimes, the instructor should give students more specific guidelines to aid those inexperienced in peer response, and sometimes, the instructor might simply ask students to find the strengths and weaknesses of the paper under review. It is always valuable to give students opportunities to discuss their comments with the author and thus allow interaction and the negotiation of meaning to take place. Both face-to face interaction and technology-enhanced interaction can work. A word of caution: Varying modes for different tasks is always better than sticking to only one format all the time. The choice of which mode is better largely depends on students' needs and the actual effects of peer response on revisions.

- Apart from using different modes, maximizing the roles of participants—both students and the teacher—is crucial to the success of peer response. Students have a tendency to stick to their own comfortable roles to start with, and it is the instructor who needs to invite students to play different roles and to scaffold their efforts and anticipate difficulties and resolve emerging problems. For instance, some students might be excellent at providing written feedback but shy in offering criticism in face-to-face communication or on-line. Others might be the opposite. If the teacher understands his or her students' communication patterns and their preferred communication modes and styles, alternative commenting modes can be provided and different grouping strategies might be employed (see chap. 3).

- Another important consideration for the teacher in guiding students' peer response activities is that he or she should always listen to what students have to say after each activity. On-site or E-mail feedback channels should be provided, and various alternative modes should be tried. Constant feedback from students regarding their feelings and attitude toward the peer response activities they have just completed is the key to sustaining such activity. Sometimes, if students feel negative about peer response, which often happens, the teacher should stop the activity and critically assess the sources of the difficulties and try to find solutions.

- Finally, the instructor should always look for new ideas and innovative strategies to expand the modes of peer response. Classroom-oriented research, or action research in comparing the effects of different modes in peer response, and altering the roles of the teacher and the students might generate new insights into peer response. There is no one set of rules that can be used to confirm or deny which mode of peer response is better or which roles the teacher and students should play in peer response. The mode of choice largely depends on the dynamics of the group, instruction in peer response activities, specific task requirements, and above all, constant communication between the teacher and the students and among the students themselves.

# Chapter 5
## Foci of Peer Response

This chapter addresses the important issue of what students should focus on when responding to their peers' drafts. Should students focus on content, rhetoric, or grammar? Or should the focus be on a combination of any two or all three? Many writing teachers, both L1 and L2, agree that the most helpful comments for student revision are those that address global issues such as content and rhetoric as specifically as possible. For example, rather than pointing out a grammatical error, a more helpful comment on a draft might focus on audience or organization. However, the comments should be specific enough to enable the writer to understand why the reader has a question so that the writer is able to revise the problem. In other words, if there is a problem with the thesis statement being unclear, a helpful specific comment would pinpoint why the statement is too unclear (e.g., "After reading your thesis statement I am not sure if you are going to discuss the problems of air pollution or the solutions"), rather than providing a more general statement (e.g., "Your thesis statement is unclear"). But are students able to provide specific comments about rhetoric and content, or do they tend to focus mostly on surface errors of grammar or style?

Overall, there is some indication that for both L1 and L2 writers, it is more common to focus on surface errors (Beason 1993; Berger 1990; Leki 1990; Yagelski 1995), perhaps because of lack of confidence in pointing out rhetorical or content-based concerns. However, a great number of studies have also shown that both L1 and L2 writers, especially those who have been trained in peer response, are able to pick out content and rhetorical problems (Berg 1999; Berger 1990; Caulk 1994; Dreyer 1992; Hansen 2001; Hansen and Liu 2000; Hedgcock and Lefkowitz 1992; Mendonça and Johnson 1994; Paulus 1999; Rothschild and Klingenberger 1990; Villamil and Guerrero 1998). Since it appears that students are able to focus on content-based, rhetorical, and grammatical issues to varying extents, it is important to examine which factors influence what students focus on in peer response.

A number of factors affect which type of comments students make on their peers' drafts: the students' (and the teacher's) educational background, the language of peer response, the mode of peer response, the genre of writing being discussed, the purpose of peer response, the timing of peer response, students' prior experiences with peer response, the teacher's focus in his or her own response, and the question of what is merited by the essay itself. Each of these will be briefly examined.

Some students appear to focus more on grammatical concerns. One reason for this is that their educational backgrounds are likely to have focused on grammatical issues, and as they are language learners, they may be concerned about linguistic correctness. This may be especially true in foreign language contexts, where teachers are usually more concerned about grammar and idiomatic expressions in students' writing.

The language used in the peer response session may also affect what types of comments students make. Research has shown that if students use their first language, they may tend to focus more on grammar and usage, whereas if students use the second language, they may focus more on content and rhetoric (Huang 1996).

The mode of feedback may also be a factor. Many teachers are now interested in employing CALL techniques in their writing classes and employing on-line peer-reviewing software such as CommonSpace in peer response activities (see chap. 4). However, the on-line format for peer response is limited in terms of how much of the text can be presented on the screen at one time, which may lead students to process the text line by line. As research has found (Bloch and Brutt-Griffler 2001), this may in turn lead to greater grammatical and stylistic commentary, which peers may not find as useful. In contrast, in the traditional pen-and-paper format, comments tend to be more global in nature, as students tend to read the entire paper before commenting on the draft. In pen-and-paper format, comments can be made via symbols and connections made among different lines of the text, but in computer-based on-line reviewing, students who are not very comfortable in using software-commenting features may be confined in their comments by the format, which will lead to their doing what is feasible rather than what is necessary.

Another influence may be the *type* of writing that students are doing. It may be easier for students to focus on the content and rhetoric of essay modes such as narratives than of more difficult rhetorical modes such as persuasion (Villamil and Guerrero 1998). Instruction might also affect what students focus on in peer response. What is the stated purpose of peer response? Is it to reinforce grammar? Rhetorical conventions? Probe and flesh out the content? Whatever guidelines the teacher sets up—whether orally or written, explicit or implicit, modeled or described—students are likely to adhere to them when responding to peers' drafts.

This relates to another instructional factor—the timing of peer response. In instructional settings where the process approach to writing—with stages roughly corresponding to brainstorming, writing the first draft, revising content and organization for the second draft, and editing for the final draft—is commonplace, such as in many educational settings in the United States, the timing of peer response activities may implicitly (or explicitly) signal to students what they should focus on in revision. Therefore, if peer response activities take place after the first draft, students may naturally focus more on content and organizational patterns; if they are before the final draft, students may tend to focus more on editing concerns.

Students' prior experiences with peer response are also a factor. Whether positive or negative, students' perceptions about peer response are derived to a great extent from their prior experiences with this type of activity (see chap. 1). If they have never experienced peer response activities before, then they may not be sure about what is expected of them or what to focus on and may follow their peers' lead. If they have experienced peer response in the past, then what they were asked to focus on previously will probably have an impact on what they focus on in subsequent peer response activities.

Students also tend to follow their teacher's lead in commenting on peers' drafts. If the teacher typically comments on grammatical issues when responding to students' papers, then it is likely that students will also focus more on grammatical issues when responding to peers' drafts. After all, as teachers of the writing process we also model writing, revising, and editing behaviors, whether intentionally or not. Therefore, if we want students to focus on a particular issue, then we also have to provide them with examples of this type of behavior by modeling this focus of response ourselves.

Finally, what the paper itself needs in terms of revision may influence what students comment on. For example, even if we ask our students to focus on content when reading their peers' drafts, they may find it difficult to avoid commenting on obvious grammatical errors and/or misspellings. Conversely, if we ask students to focus on editing issues when responding, they may have a difficult time focusing only on editing issues if there are problems with meaning or if the organizational pattern is unclear.

The fact that there are numerous factors that can influence the peer response process does not mean that what students focus on is beyond the teacher's (and students') control. In fact, the teacher can guide students to focus on different elements of writing, as the following discussion of the foci of peer response will illustrate. Through instructing students in peer response (see chap. 6) and providing models, teachers can develop peer response activities that meet both class and individual instructional needs.

One last note before we discuss the foci of peer response: Two seemingly important factors are noticeably missing from the discussion of factors influencing what students focus on in peer response activities—age and proficiency level. While these two factors may appear to have an impact on what students focus on, they in fact do not have to play a large role in determining foci. Younger learners, as well as adults, can focus on content, rhetoric, and grammar (Peregoy and Boyle 1990; Samway 1987; Urzúa 1987), as can students at all proficiency levels. The guiding tenets in designing peer response activities, no matter the age or proficiency level, are that the activities have a *purpose* (e.g., that there is a reason to focus on content); that they provide learners with *opportunities to extend their current level of competence* through collaborative learning and scaffolding; and that they *match instructional and learner objectives.*

Content, rhetoric/organization, grammar/style, and a combination of foci will now be discussed, the following questions guiding the discussion. Can students focus on a particular concern? What is the purpose of the focus? What kind of focus should students have? When should students focus on a particular concern? How can we facilitate their focus?

## Focus on Content

### Can students focus on content?

The first question to be explored is whether students can focus on content when they respond to their peers' drafts. While some researchers have found that some students may have difficulty in focusing on content (e.g., Leki 1990; Nelson and Murphy 1992, 1993), other researchers have found that students can point out concerns with, question, and give suggestions on content (Berg 1999; Berger 1990; Caulk 1994; Dreyer 1992; Hansen 2001; Hansen and Liu 2000; Hedgcock and Lefkowitz 1992; Mendonça and Johnson 1994; Paulus 1999; Rothschild and Klingenberger 1990; Villamil and Guerrero 1998). In fact, in L2 research comparing the comments made by teachers and by peers in peer response sessions, it has been shown that students, including basic or beginning writers, focus more on content and rhetorical concerns than teachers and that teacher comments tend to focus more on grammatical concerns than rhetorical or content issues (Caulk 1994; Connor and Asenavage 1994; Hedgcock and Lefkowitz 1992; Paulus 1999). Furthermore, one study found that students' comments were more specific, and therefore more useful for revision, than teachers' comments (Caulk 1994) (see chap. 1). In research on peer response in advanced writing classes in higher education, Belcher (1990) also found that when students were grouped by major, they were able to give more specific and useful content-focused comments than the teacher.

## What is the purpose of focusing on content?

Why should teachers guide students toward focusing on content? The first and most obvious reason is for topic development in terms of expansion (or reduction) of content and clarification of content. Even the most carefully planned papers by writers at all proficiency levels benefit from a peer reading (as indeed most professional papers do, including this book!)—to check whether meaning is clear, concepts have been explained clearly, and examples have been provided. The writer may understand her or his meaning clearly, but there is no guarantee that another reader will. Therefore, on the most obvious level, peer response that focuses on content is an important tool in helping writers become more aware of topic development.

There are also several other rationales for focusing on content in peer response. If students focus on content in peer response after writing the first draft, this helps to reinforce the process approach to writing. From a sociocultural perspective, employing peer response activities that focus on meaning helps students share their experiences, ideas, and backgrounds, whether the papers are narratives about personal experiences (e.g., "My Favorite Day," for younger learners) or field-specific essays in advanced writing classes. As students share their ideas, thoughts, and even information about their major fields of study, social interaction is promoted, and support networks in class may be created. In fact, this type of activity closely resembles the many "icebreaker" activities teachers employ at the beginning of every semester/course/ school year with the objective of developing social relationships among learners and group cohesion in class. Therefore, focus on content in peer response can be an effective pedagogical tool and also an effective sociocultural and affective tool in establishing support systems among students. This may be especially relevant in courses in which ESL students are in the minority, such as in mainstream K–12 classes in which students receive ESL pullout instruction but otherwise are placed in regular content courses in the regular curriculum and in mixed sections of English composition courses at the university level.

Finally, another reason to employ content-focused peer response activities is to promote collaborative learning in terms of content—in other words, as a means of content-based instruction. A focus on content in peer response activities can be effectively employed at all levels of writing proficiency and at all grade levels to foster content-knowledge development. For example, in a middle school class, students might be working on research projects on various topics, such as "American Presidents." Rather than having the teacher provide all the information or having all the materials come from a textbook, students can be assigned to research different presidents and create independent research projects. The peer response activity then becomes one way of sharing knowledge. (Students might also give presentations, post information, or publish their papers as chapters in a book on American presidents.) Content-based peer response activities then become ways of managing content in instruction (especially relevant in bilingual education settings); giving students confidence as language learners as they become the "experts" on their topic; and providing opportunities for scaffolding, negotiation of meaning, and collaborative learning as students become peer-tutors in helping their classmates acquire new content knowledge.

## What kind(s) of content should students focus on?

We make a distinction between surface and deep content. If students focus on surface content, they may have a general understanding of the paper without necessarily understanding the writer's intent and the deeper issues of how and why an action happened or of how ideas are connected. In contrast, if students have a deeper understanding of a paper, they are able to make connections among ideas and to follow the writer's logic, implicit meaning, and intent.

In order to give students better feedback for use in revisions, it is more helpful to have students focus on deeper-meaning issues in each other's papers. This may be difficult in some instances, however—such as in advanced writing courses in higher education when students are writing about topics in their fields of study. In these cases, students can be grouped by major/field of study in order to facilitate content understanding. In such a case, and in content-focused peer response activities in other classroom scenarios, it may be possible to direct students toward a deeper assessment of the writing—in other words, toward a critical reading of the paper—by giving them guided questions that challenge, explore, and probe the writer's ideas, meanings, and intent. For example, rather than asking students to give general comments on meaning (e.g., "Was the meaning of essay clear?"), which does not challenge the reader to read for a deeper understanding, students can be asked to respond to questions such as, "How was the writer able to establish the importance of $X$?"

### When should students focus on content?

Since the purpose of focusing on content is to facilitate the revision of meaning—clarification of ideas—the typical time for focusing on content is after the first draft. This allows students to focus on meaning before focusing on form—in other words, not to be hindered in their exploration of content by grammatical constraints. Additionally, focusing on content after the first draft helps reinforce the usual stages of the writing process.

However, there are several complications with this. First of all, not all writers follow the "traditional" process approach to writing that most textbooks advocate (i.e., brainstorming, drafting, revising, and editing). So, while focusing on content after the first draft may fit neatly within this process and will probably work for many writers, it is not necessarily a perfect match for all students' writing processes. That is not to say, however, that most writers will not benefit from a focus on content at this stage; it may mean that we have to be flexible and allow students to focus on other concerns, such as grammar, if they feel that they are constrained in meaning by difficulties in form. Second, a focus on content after the first draft also implies, correctly or not, that this is the only time we focus on content. Of course, that is not necessarily true. Content should be a recurring focus, based on needs, throughout the entire writing process; it may be that there is a *stronger* focus on content at this initial stage, followed by a stronger focus on form at later stages, depending on what the paper needs.

### How can we facilitate students' focusing on content?

How can we facilitate students' focusing on content, especially the deeper-content focus that may lead to better revisions? Instruction is essential (see chap. 6), as is the teacher's modeling of the response behavior that students are expected to follow. Finally, in initial peer response activities in a given class, structured peer response sheets may help students read the paper more carefully and focus on deeper-meaning issues. These peer response sheets can be written beforehand by the teacher or, alternatively, developed by individual groups and/or the whole class. In fact, having students create the peer response sheets themselves (with the teacher monitoring) may be an excellent way to help them begin thinking about the important elements in focusing on meaning. The questions in table 8 exemplify what a teacher may want students

**TABLE 8.   Probing Questions for Focusing on Content**

| Genre | Probing Questions |
|---|---|
| General (across all genres) | What was your favorite part of this paper? Why? What did you learn about X after reading this paper? What most impressed you about the paper? |
| Narrative | Who was the narrator of the story? Can you clearly describe the narrator? Do you think it is important to be able to describe the narrator for this story? Why or why not? How important is the narrator to the story? How does the narrator feel about the events of the story? How do you know? If you aren't sure, do you think the writer needs to make it clear? Why or why not? How can the writer make it clear? |
| Process ("How-to") | Why does the writer want you to know how to do X? How does the writer establish this purpose? |
| Argument | What was your position on X before reading this paper? After reading this paper? If your feelings changed as a result of reading this paper, describe what made you change your feelings. If you disagreed with the author and you didn't change your feelings, what do you think the writer could have done differently to be more persuasive? If you already agreed with the author before reading the paper, how do you think your ideas affected how you read this paper? What evidence was especially persuasive? What evidence did not have any impact on you? Why? |
| Description | What senses did the writer employ in describing X? Could you taste, feel, smell, hear, and see X? What did you want to see, feel, smell, hear, and taste that you didn't? What was the most vivid? What senses were underdeveloped? |

to focus on in reading in order to aid them in responding to content. These probing questions are organized by some possible genres and can be appropriately simplified according to grade level, age, and proficiency level of students, as well as used as models to develop questions for other genres.

## Focus on Rhetoric and Organization

### Can students focus on rhetoric and organization?

Similar to research that indicates that students can focus on content when responding to their peers' writing, research (e.g., Berg 1999; Berger 1990; Caulk 1994; Dreyer 1992; Hansen 2001; Hansen and Liu 2000; Hedgcock and Lefkowitz 1992; Mendonça and Johnson 1994; Paulus 1999; Rothschild and Klingenberger 1990; Villamil and Guerrero 1998) also indicates that students can focus on rhetoric and organization in peer response. Even young learners have been shown to be able to focus on rhetorical and organizational issues in peer response (Samway 1987; Urzúa 1987).

### What is the purpose of focusing on rhetoric and organization?

First of all, as with the focus on content, the obvious answer is that as students are still in the process of developing an understanding of different rhetorical and organizational patterns, focus on these issues in peer response may be necessary in order to help writers structure their papers more clearly. In other words, the paper may need rhetorical and organizational revision.

Additionally, there are a number of other justifications for focusing on rhetoric and organization. For one thing, it serves as a reinforcement of what the students are learning in class in terms of different structural patterns, which, though not the only important aspects of rhetoric, are important. In this sense, focusing on rhetoric also becomes a collaborative learning activity, in which students help each other probe and expand their knowledge. For students who have advanced literacy skills in their native language, peer response also allows for a type of rhetorical consciousness-raising that helps them to develop a metalinguistic awareness of rhetoric, and especially contrastive rhetoric, in terms of how their own knowledge of L1 rhetorical patterns influences their reading and writing of L2 patterns. Ultimately, this can enable students to become better monitors of their own writing in the L2 and can foster an awareness of the different rhetorical demands of different kinds of writing (and of writing in different languages), ideally without forcing students to subjugate their own prior literacy practices.

## What kind of rhetoric and organization should students focus on?

Since the rhetorical and organizational patterns students employ in writing a specific paper typically result from an instructional focus on these types of patterns, the type of rhetoric and organization that students focus on in peer response necessarily results from instructional objectives—in other words, from which patterns are meant to be practiced. Additionally, across all types of writing, it may be helpful to have students focus on some recurring, and possibly still difficult, issues such as topic sentences, thesis statements, concluding paragraphs, or concluding sentences. A continuing focus on these aspects of rhetoric across writing modes may have several instructional objectives.

1. It offers a spiraling approach to instruction so that students are exposed to the same concepts several times, since learning is not a linear process and since some students may still struggle with these constructs by semester's end.
2. It exposes learners to a greater variety of choices—in, for example, how topic sentences can be written and where

they are placed—which can help them expand their current knowledge.

3. It allows for some individualization in terms of tailoring peer response to fit the needs of different learners by offering options of what to focus on in a specific paper based on the writer's needs.

## When should students focus on rhetoric and organization?

Since rhetoric and organization are global concerns in writing (as opposed to local concerns, such as grammar, although some grammatical errors can also be considered global if they interfere with meaning), they are logically addressed in the initial stages of writing. Therefore, a focus on rhetoric and organization is often collapsed with a focus on content in the initial draft. However, as with content, a focus on rhetoric and organization need not be, and arguably should not be, limited to only the first draft, since these types of revisions may be daunting and difficult for writers to make and, as a result, problems can linger throughout the writing process. Therefore, it may be best to focus on content and rhetoric after the first draft and then check these aspects again in later peer response activities.

## How can we facilitate students' focusing on rhetoric and organization?

The most effective way to ensure that students focus on rhetoric and organization is to model this focus, give them practice with it, and develop guide sheets for each genre of writing. A sample of the kinds of questions that can be used for some rhetorical modes and for overall organization is given in table 9. These questions can be modified and simplified based on the needs of students, and used to develop questions for other rhetorical modes not illustrated here.

**TABLE 9.  Probing Questions for Focusing on Rhetoric and Organization**

| Genre | Probing Questions |
|---|---|
| General (across all genres) | Can you clearly state what the author's main idea is for this paragraph?<br>Where is the main idea?<br>How do you know it is the main idea?<br>If it isn't clear, what do you think the writer could do to make her or his main idea clearer?<br>Does the writer signal the end of the paper?<br>What words does she or he use?<br>Was it effective?<br>Why or why not? |
| Narrative | Read the first sentence of the story.<br>After you read this sentence, what do you predict the story will be about?<br>Read the rest of the story.<br>Was your prediction correct?<br>Why not?<br>How does the story end?<br>Did the ending surprise you?<br>Why or why not?<br>Do you think the ending was clearly connected to the story? |
| Process ("How-to") | If you had to follow the writer's instructions to make $X$, could you?<br>Why or why not?<br>What signals does the writer use to show the order of the steps?<br>What words could the writer use to make the steps easier to follow?<br>Where should the writer put them? |
| Argument | Was the writer's position on $X$ clear?<br>Describe what made it clear.<br>If it wasn't clear, how would you rewrite it to make it clearer?<br>When (where in the paper) did you realize what position the writer had on $X$?<br>Was this too early/late?<br>Can this be moved anywhere else?<br>What would be the effect if it were moved? |

## Focus on Grammar and Style

### Can students focus on grammar?

Research has shown that students can focus on grammar when reading their peers' papers (e.g., Caulk 1994; Connor and Asenavage 1994; Hansen 2001; Hansen and Liu 2000; Hedgcock and Lefkowitz 1992; Huang 1996; Paulus 1999). Younger learners are also able to focus on grammar when responding to their peers' papers (Peregoy and Boyle 1990). In fact, grammatical concerns may be the most common focus for both L1 and L2 writers in peer response (Beason 1993; Berger 1990; Leki 1990; Yagelski 1995).

### What is the purpose of focusing on grammar?

The focus on grammar in peer response is not without controversy, due largely to the fact that many students focus on grammar in peer response at the expense of a focus on content and rhetoric. However, that does not mean that focusing on grammar is not important. With instruction, students can be guided to focus on content and rhetoric in initial drafts and then focus on grammar in subsequent drafts for final editing. As Beason (1993) points out, grammar corrections are not negative—they do help linguistic development. Additionally, they (1) show teachers the learners' levels of metalinguistic knowledge; (2) allow peers to learn, via scaffolding, from their peers; and (3) help raise students' awareness of grammar through a critical reading of the text. Even in reading papers by advanced L2 writers, some subject-matter instructors have to correct grammatical mistakes before they can actually comment on content. Furthermore, grammatical errors may be among the most prevalent writing problems students face, and the most difficult to correct. Of course, grammatical comments alone may not help students revise their papers if there are rhetorical or content areas that need to be examined; however, they should not be viewed negatively or discouraged.

In helping students focus on grammar, teachers can do a number of things:

1. conduct peer response activities over a number of drafts and focus on rhetorical/content concerns for the first draft and then grammatical/stylistic concerns on subsequent drafts;
2. encourage students to focus on global issues overall but allow them to make grammatical corrections if poor grammar interferes with meaning; and
3. provide worksheets that focus on specific concerns for the peer response activities but also allow flexibility in commentary so that students can address both global and local issues.

Finally, focusing on grammatical errors within the context of peer response activities does provide a meaningful, context-embedded examination of form—one that may lead to long-term language development, in contrast with grammatical lessons that are not necessarily connected to students' immediate communicative needs (H. D. Brown 2001).

## What kind of grammar should students focus on?

Since a focus on grammar in peer response should best be viewed as an opportunity not just for editing but for overall linguistic development, the type of grammar to focus on has to be linked to both instructional objectives and individual needs. That is, students should be guided to focus on the grammatical points that are a focus of instruction, based on the teacher's perceptions of students' linguistic needs and their level of development, and that are individually tailored to meet the needs of each student—in other words, to help focus their attention on their typical and consistent error patterns and thus provide consciousness-raising opportunities. Of course, the issue of global versus local grammatical errors is also important. If there are grammatical errors that appear to interfere with meaning (e.g., clause structure), those are priority errors to focus on; those grammatical mistakes that may not interfere with overall comprehensibility (e.g., errors with prepositions and articles) may not be a priority in peer response. However it is important to keep in mind that when global errors are few, students may benefit from feedback on local errors (especially if this type of feedback is rare). Additionally, we also have to respect the wishes of the writer. While local errors may not create errors in understanding, they may be annoying to a reader (and to the writer) and also stigmatize the writer as "nonnative." Some writers, especially those at advanced levels, may want specific feedback on all types of errors in order to move beyond their current level of competence.

### When should students focus on grammar?

Peer response activities that focus on grammar usually take place before the final draft, as a natural part of the editing process in the process approach to writing. The justification for this placement is that students should focus first on meaning without being hindered in expressing their ideas by concerns about grammatical correctness. However, we may need to allow for some flexibility in terms of when students should focus on grammar if there are global errors that interfere with meaning. Also, an argument can be made that surface issues may need to be taken care of first to allow for a focus on meaning and organization (i.e., so that a reader is not distracted from the meaning because of consistent grammatical, stylistic, and spelling errors). Therefore, while a focus on editing and grammatical/stylistic needs (i.e., more local errors) should be delayed until the meaning is clear, there may need to be *some* focus on grammar, especially global errors, earlier in the response process in order to make sure that meaning can become clear. In other words, there may not be a clear dichotomy between meaning and form, and a strict policy of not focusing on grammar until the final draft may in fact be detrimental to meaning.

### How can we facilitate students' focusing on grammar?

A focus on grammar should reinforce instruction and help learners develop a metalinguistic awareness of their own error patterns so that they are enabled, to some extent, to edit their own work for these errors. Therefore, we suggest the following:

- The teacher should focus on only a few types of grammatical/stylistic issues per peer response activity to make grammar more manageable.
- The teacher should focus the grammar review on what students have already been instructed on in class in order to reinforce instruction.
- As the teacher becomes aware of learners' error patterns, she or he should do a minilesson on a selected pattern and have the students focus on that pattern in responding to each other's papers.
- During and after peer response activities, the teacher should have students keep a journal that lists the errors they made and how to correct them. The students should then check through the journal as they read their own papers in the future in order to monitor their own error patterns and become self-sufficient in editing.

### Focus on a Combination of Features

### Can students focus on a combination of features?

The answer to this question is Yes (e.g., Berg 1999; Berger 1990; Caulk 1994; Dreyer 1992; Hansen 2001; Hansen and Liu 2000; Hedgcock and Lefkowitz 1992; Mendonça and Johnson

1994; Paulus 1999; Rothschild and Klingenberger 1990; Villamil and Guerrero 1998). In fact, the natural tendency in peer response *is* to focus on a combination of features, especially if students are trained, since this is what the paper may need and what may best facilitate effective revisions by the writer.

### What is the purpose of focusing on a combination of features?

It is important to consider to what extent different kinds of commentary are in fact necessary on a student's paper and what is the most productive focus in responding to the first draft and subsequent drafts. For the most part, it may be more constructive to focus on content, rhetoric/organization, and any global grammatical errors that impede meaning in the first draft and then on editing and stylistic concerns in the final draft. Of course, as mentioned earlier, focusing on content and rhetoric/organization on the first draft does not mean that all these problems will be corrected. In addition, corrections in themselves may lead to other problems in content and rhetoric/organization that will need to be focused on in the editing phase (which may or may not be a true editing phase, since the assumption that all the comments made by the teacher and students are automatically adopted is not legitimate). Therefore, it may be necessary to focus on a combination of features across all drafts.

### What combination of features should students focus on, and when should students focus on a combination of features?

Since it may be necessary to focus on content, rhetoric/organization, and grammar across all drafts—perhaps more conducive to learning in any case—a suggested time line for a two-draft peer response activity is given in table 10. If students turn in three drafts before the final paper, then peer response may still focus primarily on content and organiza-

**TABLE 10. Time Line for a Combination of Foci**

| Draft | Primary Foci | Secondary Foci |
|---|---|---|
| First | Content<br>    Enough? Well-developed?<br>    Clear? Consistent? Redundant?<br><br>Rhetoric/organization<br>    Topic sentence? Conclusion?<br>    Clear organization? Cohesion? | Grammar<br>    Any unclear sentences? Words<br>    that are unclear? |
| Second | Grammar<br>    Consistent grammatical errors?<br><br>Style<br>    Spacing? Font? Paragraph<br>    format? | Content<br>    Any areas still unclear? More<br>    clarification needed?<br><br>Rhetoric/organization<br>    Topic sentence clearer? Ideas<br>    connected? Conclusion stronger? |

tion/rhetoric in the second draft and then primarily on editing issues in the final draft.

Additionally, it may be helpful to have the same person read all the drafts from one person, in order to ensure that prior problems have been dealt with, and also have an additional "new" reader read the final draft, in order to assess the overall effectiveness of the paper.

### How can we facilitate students' focusing on a combination of features?

Since it may not be possible, or necessarily justifiable, to focus on only one aspect for each draft, the following suggestions are given in order to make the peer response process manageable and effective.

### Suggestions for Teachers

- Time the different foci of peer response across the different drafts so that students focus on content and rhetoric/organization after the first draft and on grammar and style after subsequent drafts.

- If there is not sufficient time to use peer response across several drafts, then students can read each person's draft several times, focusing on one aspect each time. For example, the first time they read a paper, they can focus on meaning. The second reading can be for rhetorical/organizational issues, and the third reading can be for grammatical and stylistic issues.
- To make this more manageable, students can read a draft one section at a time—in other words, paragraph by paragraph—focusing on content, rhetoric and organization, and grammar within each paragraph. Of course, students should read the entire draft through at least once before beginning the response process.
- Work with individual students or the whole class to create peer response sheets that ask probing questions in order to facilitate a close and deep reading of and response to a text and to individualize the responses based on each writer's needs. Writers can create their own peer response sheets addressing specific concerns they have about their writing. They can be asked to develop two to three questions about meaning, two to three questions about rhetoric/organization, etc. This may be an effective way of making peer response pertinent to each student's specific needs while also reinforcing the role of the reader in the reading/writing process.
- If the focus of peer response is grammar and style, address only a few types of grammatical/stylistic issues per peer response activity in order to make grammar more manageable; focus only on what students have already learned in class in order to reinforce instruction.
- Conduct whole-class or group minilessons on different aspects of content, rhetoric, or grammar before peer response to give students the knowledge they need to successfully respond to these issues in their peers' writing.
- Have students take turns developing peer-tutoring groups on specific issues that they are comfortable

with and that they can help other students develop an awareness of.

- During and after peer response activities, have students keep a journal that lists the errors they made and how to correct them. The students should then check through the journal as they read their own papers in the future in order to monitor their own error patterns and become self-sufficient in editing.

# Chapter 6

## Instructing Students in Peer Response

Both L1 and L2 writers need to be instructed in how to respond to writing. It is not realistic to expect that our students will be able to read effectively and make constructive comments on their peers' papers without being instructed in how to do so. Nor is it reasonable to expect that our students will be able to respond constructively to the comments made by their peers on their own papers without proper instruction. Therefore, instruction in peer response is vital in forming students' perceptions toward peer response activities, the types of responses they make, and the extent to which they incorporate their peers' suggestions into their papers. In this chapter, we will discuss three major issues pertinent to peer response instruction.

First of all, why is there a need for peer response instruction? What is the rationale for instruction? Many L2 writing teachers and researchers tend to ignore or downplay the role of peer response activities in their classrooms simply because peer response has little effect on students' revisions of their drafts; they tend to perceive peer response activities themselves as being at fault without questioning what they do to prepare their students for such activities. Needless to say, questioning the effects of peer response without questioning the adequacy of peer response instruction is misleading.

Second, what is supposed to be covered in peer response instruction, or what is the content of peer response instruction? Where shall we start, and how shall we incorporate such instruction into the entire process of writing instruction? What are the procedures for instruction? What aspects of instruction should we cover? What are the responsibilities of the teacher and of the students?

Third, at what stage of writing instruction should we incorporate students' peer response activities, or what should the timing of peer response instruction be? In order to maximize the role of peer response, we have to consider when our students should receive their peers' comments and also their teacher's comments. What is the role of teachers in peer response activities? Will the teacher's presence help make sure students are on the right track, or will the teacher's presence inhibit students' participation and group interaction? Should peer response instruction be completed before students actually participate in peer response, or should we train our students in peer response one step at a time? There are no simple answers to these questions, but there are some guidelines that teachers can use to make informed decisions and offer students the necessary instruction in order to maximize the effect of peer response activities.

A brief note before we begin: Instruction can be a time-consuming activity. To many teachers, instruction and peer response may appear daunting, since they seem to necessitate too great a time commitment. However, it is important to note that instruction and peer response activities are beneficial for students (see chap. 1) and improve not only draft quality but also the overall language skills of students. It is important to engage students in peer response activities in order to help them develop their writing skills, but instructors need to invest time in instruction to ensure a high return on these activities. Proper instruction results in better peer response activities, which in turn result in higher-quality writing from students.

## The Rationale for Instruction

The importance of peer response has been acknowledged by both L1 and L2 writing researchers (Berg 1999; Ferris and Hedgcock 1998; Guerrero and Villamil 1994; Hansen and Liu

2000; Hedgcock and Lefkowitz 1992; Hirvela 1999; Liu 1997, 1998; Mangelsdorf 1989; Mittan 1989; Stanley 1992; Villamil and Guerrero 1996, 1998). As far as the L1 literature is concerned, the difference between what happens when students are instructed in peer response versus what happens when they are not instructed is obvious in several ways.

Inexperienced writers and readers often get caught up in the subject of an essay and end up spending a lot of time discussing ideas rather than how these ideas are presented and expressed in writing. When students are not instructed in peer response, some of their verbal responses can be useless, uninformed, and nonconstructive because these verbal responses seldom allow students to contemplate their reactions and word them appropriately (Huff and Kline 1987).

To investigate the effects of instruction in university freshman composition classes (eight sections with 169 participants) over the course of one 15-week semester, Zhu (1995) compared participants in an experimental group and in a control group, each of which consisted of four sections. The experimental group was instructed via teacher-student conferences in which the teacher met students in groups of three to develop and practice strategies for peer response, whereas participants in the control group received no systematic instruction—aside from viewing a video example—regarding quantity and quality of feedback or student interaction during peer response sessions. Analyses of data indicated that instructing students led to significantly more and higher-quality peer feedback and livelier discussions in the experimental group. This study also revealed that there seemed to be a relationship between the extent of negotiated meaning and peer feedback: When there was negotiation, peer feedback tended to be more specific. On the other hand, when there was no negotiation, feedback tended to be more general.

Instructed students tend to make more revisions directly resulting from peer response, and instruction also results in a greater level of student engagement in the task of evaluation, in more productive communication about writing, and in clearer guidelines for the revision of drafts (Stanley 1992). In a recent study comparing two groups of ESL students, with one group receiving instruction and the other receiving no instruction for peer response, Berg (1999) found that instruction appeared to account for greater improvement in revised drafts. Berg also found that students instructed in peer response improved their writing from a first to a second draft more than uninstructed students. Moreover, the findings of the study indicated that the relative effects of instruction in peer response on writing outcomes were not influenced by the students' levels of writing proficiency.

Although it is understood that the effectiveness of peer response activities is partly due to adequate preparation on the part of the students, writing teachers might find it hard to locate resources and/or information on how to prepare their students to become proficient peer responders. Therefore, detailed information and guidelines in instructing our students to become effective peer responders are needed, as is a synthesis of what has been found effective by those who have had successful experiences in their classrooms. Such information will aid those who are interested in using peer response activities in their classrooms in adapting these activities to their own educational demands.

## Instruction for Responding

When we talk about instruction, we need first of all to ask ourselves two fundamental questions: (1) Who needs to be instructed? and (2) What is instruction?

The first question deals with our own belief system about peer response. It is hard for us to instruct our students in peer response if we do not believe in it ourselves. That is, if we do not believe that peer response is a useful way to help students negotiate meaning and forms and will help them make subsequent revisions of their writing, then the instruction we can offer to our students is questionable from the outset. The instruction starts with our beliefs. Some of us might not have experience with peer response, or might not have had positive experiences with peer response, but that should not affect our own attitudes toward instruction. We should first train ourselves to be open-minded and to challenge our own beliefs and attitudes toward peer response activities. Although learning how to respond to the work of their peers is a task students share with their writing teachers, teachers have the responsibility to provide a supportive atmosphere conducive to successful peer response and to provide concrete guidelines useful in the process of peer response. Students have the responsibility to know exactly what to do before, during, and after peer response activities.

But what is instruction, and what should be included in the guidelines? Based on her own classroom teaching experiences, Berg (1999) developed 11 guidelines for ESL teachers to use in training students in peer response. Each is supported by her personal experiences and her observations as a teacher. They are summarized as follows (Berg 1999, 21).

1. Create a comfortable classroom atmosphere that promotes trust among students by conducting a number of in- and out-of-class, get-to-know-you activities.
2. Establish the role of peer response in the writing process and explain the benefits of having peers, as opposed to just teachers, respond to students' writing.
3. Highlight the common purpose of peer response among professional and student writers by examining the acknowledgments in textbooks and other publications, and discuss how both ask others to read their work.
4. Demonstrate and personalize the peer response experiences by displaying several drafts of a text written by someone the students know that demonstrate how peer comments helped improve the writing.
5. Conduct a collaborative, whole-class response activity using a text written by someone unknown to students, and stress the importance of revising the clarity and rhetorical level aspects rather than sentence-level errors.
6. Address issues of vocabulary and expressions by comparing inappropriate comments with appropriate ones.

7. Familiarize students with a response sheet by showing samples and explaining its purpose as a tool designed to help them focus on important areas of the writing assignment.

8. Involve students in a response to a collaborative writing project by having them use the peer response sheet to respond as pairs or groups to a paragraph written by another group of students. Based on the responses, have the pairs or groups then revise their original collaborative paragraphs.

9. Allow time for questions and expressions of concern by talking to students about their writing, the peer responses, the revisions they made, the difficulties in judging classmates' comments, and lack of confidence in their revision abilities.

10. Provide revision guidelines by highlighting good revision strategies and explaining that peer response helps authors understand the difference between intended and perceived meaning.

11. Study examples of successful and unsuccessful peer response using videotapes or printed samples to examine level of student engagement, language used, and topics discussed.

Lin and Sadler (2000) replicated these guidelines in an undergraduate ESL composition class at a Southwestern U.S. university. Based on their experiences, they added four points they found important in instruction.

12. To increase the responsibility of students in peer response, instructors should read peer comments based on peer response sheets and give students credit for their comments.

13. Students should be given ample opportunities to familiarize themselves with *what* to comment on (e.g., peer response sheets) and also *how* to make comments (e.g., in on-line reviewing, the features they can use on

a computer). This is especially crucial when software such as MOO or CommonSpace is used.

14. Teachers should provide students with their comments by using the same peer response sheets later in the process so as to allow students to make revisions based on peers' comments without the intervention of the teacher. By comparing peers' comments with those from the teacher, students will be able to see the differences (not necessarily good or bad) in not only what is commented on but also how comments are made, which raises awareness of the varieties of comments and commenting strategies.

15. Students should also be given opportunities to clarify their peers' comments and exchange opinions with them before revising their drafts. This is usually done through oral peer response or on-line synchronous peer response sessions. Meanwhile, teachers should encourage their students to talk with them about their reactions toward their peers' comments on their drafts, which provides a chance to get clarification, confirmation, or reinforcement through one-on-one or group conferences with the teacher.

Finally, one of the most crucial steps in preparing students to be effective peer responders is instructing them in asking the right questions (Liu and Sadler 2000). Therefore, here is one more important point on instructing students for responding.

16. Students should be instructed in how to ask clarification questions and how to give suggestions that are revision oriented so that peer response is facilitated across affective and cognitive levels.

These 16 points are summarized in four categories in table 11 and discussed by category.

**TABLE 11. Guidelines for Preparing Students for Peer Response**

| Affective | Cognitive | Sociocultural | Linguistic |
|---|---|---|---|
| Create a comfortable environment to assist students in establishing peer trust | Highlight the purpose of peer response | Increase the awareness of the nature of intercultural communication in group work | Introduce pragmatic and useful expressions in peer response |
| | Stress the importance of peer response for revision by using drafts and peer responses to demonstrate the effects of peer response on revision | | Use examples to show what is inappropriate in peer response |
| Encourage peer support | | Invite students to reflect on their own experiences of and perceptions toward peer response work | Instruct students in asking the right questions |
| Establish the role of peer response in classrooms | Use task-specific peer response sheets catering to the needs of learners at different proficiency levels | | |
| Allow sufficient time to familiarize students with the peer response procedures and format, especially with computer software | Model the peer response process for the whole class by using videos or simulations | Introduce peer response strategies, such as turn-taking, interaction, showing respect to peers, etc. | |
| Give peer comments before those from the teacher | Provide concrete revision guidelines based on peer responses | | |
| | Practice asking questions that encourage negotiation of meaning | | |

## Creating a Positive Classroom Atmosphere for Peer Response

Students with few or no experiences in peer response might easily get frustrated or intimidated in communicating with peers whom they do not know very well or whose cultural and linguistic backgrounds might be different from their own. One of the problems most teachers encounter is that students in a given group might not feel comfortable in critiquing others' papers for fear that the writers might not receive their criticism well. As a result, there is silence instead of discussion.

On the other hand, some students might be too critical of their peers' papers and tend to dominate the entire discussion, leaving those who have something to contribute to the discussion no opportunity to express their ideas. As students' motivation to participate in peer response activities is affected, they will gradually form negative attitudes toward these activities.

One solution to this problem is to create a comfortable environment where students have opportunities to get to know one another in terms of their linguistic and sociocultural backgrounds, majors of study, communication styles, and personalities. Some warm-up "getting to know you" activities in a group, such as having students interview each other about family backgrounds or play games to learn some personal characteristics besides names, could be helpful. Before students are asked to critique each other's work, the teacher can familiarize students with the peer response process and peer response formats by using a sample draft from a previous class and engaging students in making group comments on that draft. Another option is to give students some group assignments, such as describing a problem using a thesis statement, to allow group members to collaborate in order to build peer trust, which we know is conducive to effective peer response activities.

When peer response software is used or peer response is conducted through an on-line synchronous communication mode (see the detailed discussion later in this chapter and see chap. 4), teachers will need to be sensitive to the students' anxiety levels, risk-taking abilities, and inhibitions. We should allow students ample time and opportunities to "play around" with the software until they feel comfortable using whatever is introduced. If students are required to use software for peer response activities, lab tutorials or detailed written guidelines should be provided in order to meet the individual needs of students. The success of peer response activities lies in the collaboration of every member of a group; we as teachers have to make sure that all our students are comfortable using a given software for peer response activities.

## Instructing Students to Use Cognitive Strategies

It is usually helpful for teachers to build peer response activities into the course syllabus by highlighting the purpose of peer response in the process of writing. The more emphasis we put on peer response activities in L2 writing classes, the better prepared our students will be before they start engaging in peer response. Lockhart and Ng (1995) point out that teachers should make it immediately clear that the purpose of peer response is not only to help writers revise their texts but also to develop both readers' and writers' critical skills for analyzing writing. Therefore, students should be encouraged to be "supportive to each other and to focus on how meaning is conveyed throughout the text" (Lockhart and Ng 1995, 613). It has also been found effective to stress the importance of peer response for revision by showing students actual drafts and peer responses (Berg 1999). This can be done by building a portfolio of our students' drafts and the peer responses they received after the initial draft and before the final draft. Such a portfolio needs to be organized in such a way that we can find the most appropriate examples to show our current students. And, of course, we will need to have our students' consent to keep these drafts and responses on file.

For example, in teaching ESL writing courses to both undergraduate students and graduate students in a major ESL composition program at a Midwestern U.S. university, Liu created a template for data collection to be used for instructing future students in peer response. In this particular ESL program, three ESL writing courses in a sequence are offered to ESL graduate students based on their entry-level writing ability as determined by a placement test and a diagnostic essay holistically scored by trained ESL writing specialists. At each level, from lower-intermediate to upper-intermediate to advanced, students are given various assignments that typically require them to write three drafts. Peer response activities are usually implemented between students' first and second drafts to allow students to revise their first drafts based on their peers' comments without the intervention of the teacher. The teacher's comments are given to students on a later draft. As a classroom teacher researcher, Liu, with the students' consent, collected students' writings (three drafts), along with the peer responses and his own comments on students' second drafts, and identified three sets of data from each task that represented some saliency in students' revisions as the result of peer comments. Liu used these examples (some of which were later replaced with more typical ones) to train his students. Table 12 reflects the data-collection planning in the graduate sequence ESL writing classes.

In instructing students in cognitive strategies to aid them in responding to their peers' papers, it is important to guide them with task-specific peer response sheets catering to the demands and foci of each task and based on students' proficiency levels. To illustrate, Examples 1–4 show peer response sheets used in different courses. The examples are graded

**TABLE 12.  Organizing a Portfolio of Students' Sample Drafts/Peer Responses**

| Level of Students (based on writing skills) | Major Writing Tasks[a] | Drafts Required | Peer Response | Prototypes of Students' Writing Samples |
|---|---|---|---|---|
| Lower-Intermediate | A series of summaries | 2 | | Select three complete sets of students' samples (three drafts, peer |
| | A resume and cover letter | 2 | | response sheets, and |
| | *A description and analysis of a process | 3 | Between | the teacher's comments) |
| | *A comparison/contrast for the purpose of evaluation | 3 | drafts first and second | from each * task, reflecting either of the following characteristics |
| | *A discussion using cause/effect | 3 | | 1. substantial revisions (content, organization, expressions, and grammar) made by the writer as the result of peer response; |
| | | | | 2. little revision made by the writer as the result of peer response |

*(continued)*

**TABLE 12—** *Continued*

| Level of Students (based on writing skills) | Major Writing Tasks[a] | Drafts Required | Peer Response | Prototypes of Students Writing Samples |
|---|---|---|---|---|
| Upper-Intermediate | A series of summaries | 2 | | Select three complete sets of students' samples (three drafts, peer response sheets, and the teacher's comments) from each * task, reflecting either of the following characteristics: |
| | *An extended definition of a concept and the relevance of that concept to a field of study | 3 | Between drafts first and second | |
| | *A discussion of a problem and proposed solution | 3 | | 1. substantial revisions (content, organization, expressions, and grammar) made by the writer as the result of peer response; |
| | *An interpretation of discipline-specific data | 3 | | 2. little revision made by the writer as the result of peer response |
| Advanced | An annotated bibliography | 2 | | Select three complete sets of students' samples (three drafts, peer response sheets, and the teacher's comments) from each * task, reflecting either of the following characteristics: |
| | *A critical review of an article in the student's field | 3 | Between drafts first and second | |
| | *A long paper, using some citations, tailored to the student's current academic work | 3 | | 1. substantial revisions (content, organization, expressions, and grammar) made by the writer as the result of peer response; |
| | | | | 2. little revision made by the writer as the result of peer response |

[a]The asterisk indicates that a peer response is required.

---

**Example 1.  Peer Response Sheet for a "Process" Paragraph (beginning or lower-intermediate students)**

1. What is the process?

2. Is the topic sentence clear? What is it?

3. How many steps are there in the process? Can you follow them clearly? Do you think you would be able to make/do X based on these steps? Why or why not?

4. Should the writer add more steps or delete steps? Which ones and why?

5. Are there signal words before each step? Should the writer add more?

6. How does the writer end the paragraph? Should the writer change the ending?

7. What other suggestions do you have for the writer?

---

from sheets that may be appropriate for students in community college courses or in intensive English programs (Examples 1 and 2) to sheets more appropriate to courses that focus on writing for academic purposes, such as undergraduate or graduate ESL courses (Examples 3 and 4).

We also have to remember that giving peer response sheets to students is only part of our job. As teachers, we have to model the peer response process for the whole class by using the same response sheets we want our students to use. Such a demonstration should be included in peer response instruction. One way to do this is to show students a draft and the peer responses on the task-specific peer response sheet and then to offer evaluations not only of *what* comments are appropriate but also of *how* these comments are constructed.

Finally, students need instruction in asking the types of questions that will lead to clarification and therefore in-

**Example 2.  Peer Response Sheet for a "Problem/Solution" Essay (intermediate or upper-intermediate students)**

1. What is the thesis statement of the essay? Does it clearly state what this essay is about? Why or why not?

2. Does the writer give enough background information to the problem in the introduction? What else could he or she add?

3. What three solutions does the writer suggest? Are these solutions realistic? Why or why not? Can you think of any other solutions the writer might add?

4. What examples does the writer use to describe each solution? Should more be added? Why or why not?

5. How are the body paragraphs arranged? Is this organization pattern effective? Why or why not?

6. What limitations are given to each solution?

7. How did the writer conclude the essay? Was it effective?

creased negotiation of meaning, rather than giving comments that may appear critical and/or evaluative. The latter types of questions/comments may be more common in peer response, but they may have little impact on revision as they could jeopardize group cohesion by making group members anxious and defensive about their work. Having students ask the "right" questions—in other words, those that promote interaction and discussion—enables both the responders and the authors to have the opportunity to discuss specific aspects of the text; negotiate meaning (which, of course, strengthens other language skills); and work collaboratively to revise the paper. It also allows the author to have ownership of the paper while still being responsible to the reader and provides the author with concrete and specific ideas for revision.

**Example 3. Peer Response Sheet for "Definition" Task (intermediate or upper-intermediate students)**

1. What is the term being defined in this paper? Is the author's choice of a term appropriate? Can it be satisfactorily defined for a nonspecialist audience in 500 to 700 words? Is the term too simple/complex/specific/general?

2. Does the essay answer the question "What is . . . ?"?

3. After reading the essay, do you feel that you understand the term/concept reasonably well? If you do, without looking at the essay, write down in your own words a simple definition of the term/concept and explain why this term/concept is important in the author's field. If not, try to explain why you are unable to understand the author's definition.

4. Write a brief review of the paper (your review should be at least one paragraph in length). If there are any particular sections of the paper that you find difficult to follow or that you find to be very effective and well-written, be sure to point them out to the author. If you can suggest any improvements to the author, be sure to do so. As you review the paper, take into consideration not only the effectiveness of the definition but also the overall structure of the paper (e.g., Are the introduction and conclusion effective? Is the main body well organized? Does the paper contain too much, too little, or enough information?).

Table 13 outlines the possible types of questions/comments that may occur in peer response. Those that appear to be most helpful in peer response are in bold.

In terms of the area of comments, "global" refers to those comments that provide feedback on ideas, development, audience, purpose, and organization of writing, while "local" comments typically focus on grammar, style, and editing concerns. Comments that focus on evaluation include a judgment on the writing—in other words, the notion that something is "good" or "bad." Questions/comments that are considered to focus on *clarification/elaboration* ask the writer to state her or his ideas more clearly and ask/probe for details, explanations,

---

**Example 4.  Peer Response Sheet for a "Critical Review" Task (advanced students)**

1. What is your overall impression of the review? What are the main strengths and weaknesses of the review?

2. What is the organizational pattern or structure of the review (e.g., block-by-block or point-by-point)? Please sketch an outline of the critical review.

3. What criteria were employed by the writer (importance, timeliness, length, objectivity, interpretation, thoroughness, practicality, expert opinion, interest in the subject)? Were they properly used? Why or why not?

4. Please point out one or two major grammatical weaknesses of the review.

5. What are your suggestions on how to revise the paper?

---

justifications, and more information. Suggestions are comments/questions that point out directions for change, while alterations provide specific changes to be made.

The comments/questions categorized as clarification/elaboration have been known to facilitate increased negotiation of meaning and to lead to more extensive revisions; such comments generate discussion of specific elements of the text and are revision oriented in nature. Also, since they allow the writer to justify her or his perspective rather than suggesting specific changes and/or critically evaluating the text, they are also less anxiety provoking for the writer and therefore may improve group cohesion during the peer response process, which may ultimately lead the writer to take these comments into greater consideration when revising her or his paper. Additionally, unlike suggestions, alterations, and evaluation comments/questions, clarification/elaboration comments ultimately allow the writer to retain ownership of the text and responsibility for clarifying meaning for the reader, rather

**TABLE 13.    Question and Comment Types in Peer Response**

| | Global | | Local | |
|---|---|---|---|---|
| | **Revision oriented** | **Non–revision oriented** | **Revision oriented** | **Non–revision oriented** |
| Evaluation | This is not a clear thesis statement. | This is a great thesis statement. | This word does not make sense. | I like this sentence a lot. |
| **Clarification/ Elaboration** | **Could you explain your thesis statement in more detail?** | | **What do you mean by X?** | |
| Suggestion | Your thesis should be explained more clearly. | Your thesis should stay as is. | You should rephrase this sentence. | You should keep this word here. |
| Alteration | Change your thesis into X. | | Change "tail" to "tale." | |

*Source:* Liu and Sadler 2000.
*Note:* Shaded sections imply that questions/comments do not fit into the category.

than being "told" what to revise without having the opportunity to negotiate why and how.

To facilitate students' usage of clarification comments/questions, we suggest the following.

- Show students a table such as table 13 and explain the different types of comments/questions and how they affect the peer response process.
- Using a "practice draft," engage the whole class in a peer response activity and practice asking clarification questions.
- In small groups, continue instruction in how to form questions by asking students to ask each other each type of question (in other words, have them ask three to four of each type) while responding to each other's drafts. Ask them to make notes on how each of the comments made them feel and how each helped/did not help them revise

their drafts. This should be followed by a whole-class discussion about the activity and the results of being asked the different types of questions.

These activities may need to be repeated across time for reinforcement; therefore, instruction in question formation should not be seen as a one-time activity. Additionally, it may be helpful to tie this instruction to instructing students in how to use appropriate language, since there is a natural link between these two issues.

### Instructing Students to Build Sociocultural Competence

In multilingual writing classes, where students usually represent many nations across the world, L2 writing teachers face challenges in teaching a class of students with diverse linguistic and sociocultural backgrounds. These students need sociocultural competence in order to communicate with their peers from diverse backgrounds. In peer response, such competence is often regarded as one of the most important factors contributing to success. As writing teachers, we should train our students to increase their awareness of the nature of intercultural communication in group work. Such an awareness includes the ability to meet new situations with open minds. For instance, when there is disagreement about comments on a peer's paper, we should ask our students to try to be open-minded and try to respond to others in an objective way that shows respect and positive regard. Such awareness also includes *adaptability,* the ability to adapt appropriately to particular situations; *sensitivity,* the ability to convey empathy verbally and nonverbally to peers; and *creativity,* the ability to engage in divergent and systematic thinking in order to offer more constructive comments.

Another suggestion for L2 writing teachers is to invite our students to reflect on their own experiences and perceptions of peer response work through an on-line class listserv or reflection session at the end of each peer response activity. Of course, it is also very important to equip our students with a list of sociolinguistically appropriate phrases that they can use to convey their meaning.

### Instructing Students to Use Appropriate Language

A commonly observed phenomenon in peer response is that students, especially those at beginning or lower-intermediate levels, have good ideas or have realized certain weaknesses of a paper yet do not have adequate language for communicating their ideas. Although teaching formulaic language to help students with verbal communication is not highly regarded in SLA literature (Ellis 1994), it may be helpful to show students how to express themselves in a peer response session. Many ESL writers coming from EFL backgrounds, especially those from Asia, have asked us to teach them a list of phrases/sentences they can use in peer response activities. While teaching some commonly used phrases might not be the task of ESL writing teachers, we have to admit that learning how to express oneself appropriately is necessary in communication in general and in peer response activities in particular.

Sentences found to be useful among ESL writers in peer response activities appear in table 14. These are intended as suggestions to help our learners search for appropriate language as necessitated by a given context and scenario. The comments are graded by linguistic complexity, from sentences appropriate for beginning learners to those that may be more suitable for advanced learners.

### The Modes of Instruction

In practice, we should train our students to respond in three different ways: in writing, orally, and through on-line response. While the guidelines summarized earlier are helpful for peer response activities in general, we as teachers will need more concrete ideas in terms of what to do when it

**TABLE 14. Useful Sentences for Peer Response Activities**

| What ESL Students Might Say | What Might Be More Appropriate. |
| --- | --- |
| This wrong. | Is this right? |
| | I am not sure if this is right. |
| | I wonder whether this is what you had in mind? |
| | I'm afraid I don't understand what you meant. |
| | Could you explain to us what you wanted to say here? |
| | I did not quite understand your point here. Would you please rephrase the sentence? |
| How could you say that? | What do you mean here? |
| | This idea is interesting, but I could not find any discussion in your paper to support this idea. |
| | Your point is well made, but there is a lack of evidence to convince me. |
| Please change this word/ expression/sentence because it makes no sense here. | I thought this word meant . . . |
| | I don't understand this word. |
| | Could you please clarify this word/expression/ sentence? |
| | I might be wrong, but I did not catch what you meant here. |
| | Can you come up with a better word/ expression/sentence for what you had in mind? |
| I don't understand this paper. | What do you mean? |
| | What is your main idea? |
| | I'm afraid that I did not quite understand this paper because . . . |
| | It seems that you've spent a lot of time working on this paper, but could you give us a brief summary of it? |
| I don't like this paper. | I am a little confused about the paper. |
| | I am not sure I agree with your ideas. |
| | You put a lot of effort into this paper, but I feel I could have enjoyed it more if I knew what you intended to say. |
| | Although some points are well made, I guess your way of thinking is different from mine. |

*(continued)*

**TABLE 14—Continued**

| What ESL Students Might Say | What Might Be More Appropriate. |
| --- | --- |
| How could you write this paper without a thesis statement? | Can you tell me where your thesis statement is? I'm afraid that I cannot find your thesis statement. Your thesis statement is not clear to me. Could you help me locate your thesis statement in the paper? |
| Why did you use this word/ expression/sentence again and again? | Can you use another word here? You use this word a lot. Maybe use a different word. This word/expression/sentence is good here, but its power is decreased due to its overuse. I like this word/expression/sentence, but your paper might be better with a variety of expressions. Could you think of another word/expression/ sentence to enrich the text? |
| You could have done a better job. | This is good but you need to . . . I like your paper but you can . . . I can see your effort here, but I am sure you can find many ways to improve your paper, such as . . . I can see you have a lot to do in your revision of this paper, although the basic idea of this paper is there. |
| This paper is perfect. | Very good. You could . . . This is good but if you want you can . . . Well done. But this paper could be better if you . . . What a good job! If I were you, I would still work hard to improve . . . Nice job. I believe you can still work on . . . |

comes to written response instruction, oral response instruction, and on-line synchronous instruction.

### Written Peer Response

Written peer response means that students offer comments in a written format on their peers' drafts after reading them carefully. There are three types of questions commonly used on peer response sheets in ESL writing classes: *wide-open questions* (e.g., "How do you like this paper in general?" "What would you suggest that the author do to revise this draft?"); *semi-structured questions* (e.g., "Can you find the thesis statement of this draft?" "What are the main strengths and weaknesses of this draft?"); and *structured questions* (e.g., "Does the draft begin with a thesis statement?" "Does the draft have a reasonable conclusion?"). The results of studies indicate that it is usually more beneficial for students to be provided with concrete written response sheets through which they can provide clear comments. Peer response sheets usually contain a mixture of these types of questions, although students at lower proficiency levels may benefit more from structured peer response sheets than students at higher proficiency levels. For instance, Examples 5–7 show three different peer response sheets on a similar task (a problem-solution paper) for ESL writers at lower-intermediate, upper-intermediate, and advanced levels.

Sometimes it might be necessary for teachers to construct a peer response sheet containing different types of questions and information if the class includes mixed-level students. In this case, students may answer some or all of the questions, based on ability; the extent of details depends on individual students' proficiency levels. Such a generic sheet is illustrated in Example 8.

---

**Example 5.  Peer Response Sheet for a "Problem/Solution" Task (lower-intermediate students)**

1. What is the problem?

2. Is background information given to the problem?

3. What are the solutions or suggested solutions to the problem?

*Comments:* All the questions are factual, and the responders' task is to find the answers to these questions in order to reflect the clarity of the paper. If the responders' answers are different from those of the author, then the author has to revise the paper to clarify the points.

**Example 6.  Peer Response Sheet for a "Problem/Solution" Task (upper-intermediate students)**

1. How is the problem defined?

2. Explain the rhetorical devices used to present the solutions or suggested solutions to the identified problems.

3. Are there any logical connections among the solutions identified or proposed? Identify and critique the transitions used in the paper.

4. Is there a discussion about the potential results of the solutions? If so, what role does the discussion play in the paper?

*Comments:* The questions in this sheet are not only factual, but they also solicit information in terms of the readers' reactions and responses to the content and to the rhetorical devices used to convey the author's intended meaning. These questions guide the readers to look beyond the text and to examine the writing as a whole.

---

**Example 7.  Peer Response Sheet for a "Problem/Solution" Task (advanced students)**

1. What are the major strengths and weaknesses of the paper?

2. How is the paper organized? Do you believe the organization of the paper is the most appropriate based on what the author has in mind?

3. What would you do differently if you were the author? Are there any concrete suggestions you can make in terms of organization, rhetoric, grammar, and pragmatic use of language?

4. Do you believe that the problems identified and the solutions or suggestions offered are convincing?

*Comments:* The questions in this sheet are very general. They invite ideas and thoughts from readers, and some of them are demanding. But this is for advanced learners, and the questions should reflect a certain level of sophistication in thinking and responding.

**Example 8.  Peer Response Sheet for a "Problem/Solution" Task (mixed-level students)**

1. Please point out one major strength and one major weakness of the paper.

2. What is/are the problem(s) being discussed in the paper? Is it/Are they stated clearly? Please restate the problem(s) briefly.

3. Are solutions presented/recommended? Are they clear enough to possibly solve the problem(s) stated? Please outline the solutions.

4. Is there any evaluation offered? How is the evaluation related to the solution(s) to the problem(s)? Please comment on the relevance and nature of the evaluation of the paper.

5. What is the overall structural pattern of this paper in terms of various combinations of four parts—situation, problem, solution, and evaluation? Is the structure of the paper reasonable? What would you do if you were to write this paper? Please offer your rationale for the structure you think fits the topic best (either agree with the author or disagree with the author).

6. What is unclear to you in the paper? In your opinion, what should be changed, deleted, added, or restated? Please offer concrete suggestions to improve this paper.

*Comments:* This peer response sheet is detailed and provides specific directions for responding. It suits beginners who require specific information, and it also caters to intermediate and advanced-level students who can engage in reasoning and synthesis based on concrete questions.

One of the major problems with written peer response has to do with the appropriateness of the questions asked on the peer response sheet. As no set of questions can apply to all writing tasks, and as learners' linguistic and sociocultural backgrounds are so different, peer response sheets should be task-based and learner-based. If the peer response sheets are not specifically prepared by the teacher based on the learners' needs and the nature of the writing tasks, students might skip over some questions or tend to give very brief comments that are not very helpful to the writers in revising their papers.

Another problem often encountered by L2 writing teachers concerns the format of the peer response sheet. Sometimes the questions ask for more information, but the answers are scarce and brief. One reason for this could be a lack of adequate space on the peer response sheet. Although students can attach extra pieces of paper to give detailed answers, the space left between questions is indicative, in the students' minds, of the length of answers teachers expect to get. Careful design is crucial in getting enough information from students.

Written peer response sheets sometimes limit students when they have a lot to say but cannot express their ideas clearly. Students also may express their thoughts in a way the author is unable to understand. This is partly due to the linguistic abilities of the students, especially beginning or lower-intermediate writers, but their cultural backgrounds are also a factor. Whatever the reason, peer response sheets will be helpful if they are constructed in such a way that students feel they are not being asked to spend a lot of time addressing the questions on the sheet yet are able to write down what they feel strongly about. For this to happen, teachers need to show consideration for the students' time and give them enough leeway to write about the issues they feel are important. For instance, instead of asking students to point out all the weaknesses of the paper, the teacher can ask, "Among all the weaknesses of the paper in terms of organization, rhetoric, pragmatic usage, or grammar what is the most important or consistent weakness you've found in this paper?" Or, "If you were to make one suggestion to improve this paper, what would it be?" Ironically, many students will probably give more than one suggestion because the questions are phrased in a way that indicates consideration of the responders' time and because they give responders time to think over all the options/suggestions before writing down what they really feel is most important. Due to the nature of peer response, if a paper receives several responses from peers, adding all the salient suggestions together will lead the writer to a good starting point for revision. If some salient points overlap, then the need for revision is even more clear.

Written peer response sheets are also individualized so that they attend to each writer's specific needs and interests. In fact, one way of ensuring greater writer and responder investment in the peer response task and ensuing revision activities is to have writers create their own peer response sheets based on the issues they want feedback on. Students may be able to construct the entire feedback sheet by themselves or as a group, or the teacher can create guided sheets that allow some flexibility so that students can pinpoint specific areas they would like their readers to think about. Another possibility is for the teacher to construct a flexible peer response sheet that allows students to write about specific areas they would like their readers to focus on—this also helps the writers to take the readers' responses seriously and ask for clarification and specific details, since these comments are tailored to their specific needs. In a study on flexible peer response sheets, Hansen (2001) found that when students were able to coconstruct their own peer response sheets—both for peer response focusing on content and organization and peer response focusing on grammar—students were more invested in the peer response process; had a greater interest in their peers' comments (in fact, some of them were very anxious and excited to find out what their responders had suggested!); and had more favorable perceptions of the usefulness of peer response. This in turn led to more discussion and negotiation of meaning during the oral component of peer response, generating more specific comments, which ultimately led to greater and more extensive revisions on subsequent drafts.

Flexible peer response sheets can be tailored to focus on content, organization, and/or grammar, either at one time or at different stages of the writing process. Example 9 provides an illustration of a flexible peer response sheet.

### Oral Peer Response

Once peer response sheets have been exchanged among peers in a group, group members should begin the process of responding in order to give peers opportunities to highlight

**Example 9. Flexible Peer Response Sheet for a "Problem/Solution" Task (all levels)**

*Content:*

1. What did you like best about my paper? Why?

2. When you read my paper, please focus on solution number(s) _____ (writer fills this in). Do I have enough support for this solution? What support do you think I can add?

3. I had difficulty with _____. Please give me suggestions to make it more effective.

*Organization:*

4. Is the organization of my solutions effective? Which solution is the strongest? Should this solution be _____ (first, last)?

*Grammar:*

5. I am not sure how well I used _____ (semicolons, adverb phrases, etc.). Please check my use of these.

6. I also have difficulty with _____ (spelling, etc.). Please let me know if I have any errors with these.

Thank you for reading and responding to my paper! Your feedback helps a lot! ☺

and/or reinforce their written comments to the author and also to give the author a chance to ask for clarification or to offer an explanation. In a group of four students, it usually takes an entire class period of 50 minutes or an hour for all the students in a group to go through all the papers being commented on. The group leader, selected or self-selected, will make sure that there is time to go through each paper.

Instruction in oral peer response is crucial in that students who have not experienced oral critiquing before need to be equipped with appropriate expressions in order to be direct without being rude and polite without beating around the bush. Depending on the learners' oral/aural skills, teachers should show a simulated session or a videotape of a previous peer response session that covers turn-taking strategies, intercultural communication skills, proper procedures in topic initiation, negotiation of meaning, peer interaction, clarification, confirmation, and argumentation. It is not easy to teach these strategies and skills to the extent that your students can apply them in their own practice. However, it is helpful for you to raise their consciousness of these important issues in oral peer response activities. Much of the instruction is an ongoing process. The more experiences students have with peer response activities, the better communicators they will become in such group scenarios. Instruction in asking effective questions, giving effective comments, and using appropriate expressions is especially important when peer response includes an oral component.

## Computer-Mediated Peer Response

With the advancement of modern technology, more and more interactions take place through various kinds of computer-mediated communication. While the effects of using on-line peer response in teaching L2 writing are yet to be seen, the idea of using this kind of communication is becoming more fashionable and feasible. While some students, especially those from Asia, do not feel comfortable with classroom participation in the target culture (Liu 2000), it is possible that their interaction will drastically change with communication that is not face-to-face. In a recent study (Liu and Sadler 2000), students who critiqued their peers' papers by using a synchronous communication device, a MOO (see chap. 4), were compared with students who critiqued their peers' papers in a traditional face-to-face scenario. The preliminary results revealed that the comments made by the MOO group were more forceful and straightforward, while the comments made by the traditional communication group were more careful and strategic.

One of the problems of using computer software such as CommonSpace in peer response, as identified by Bloch and Brutt-Griffler (2001), is that students appeared to make fewer comments on papers than they had when commenting by hand. As for the computer's ability to facilitate the acquisition of L2 writing skills, it seemed that the computer was not inherently a good tutor. An additional problem with using computer software is that it prompted a bottom-up reading style, since text was shown on the computer screen in small chunks at a time. This appeared to encourage students to focus too much on local rather than global textual issues. However, by approaching the computer as a tool, teachers could focus on making sure that everyone uses the tool in a better way. As a result of these concerns, Bloch and Brutt-Griffler (2001) held sessions with instructors that aimed at heightening their awareness of the number and length of comments in order to counter the students' tendency to comment in a certain, possibly counterinstructive way. The constraints imposed by such CALL technology, and how instructors respond to them, certainly merit much more research.

Another problem with instruction using synchronous peer response is time constraints. Instruction in a lab takes quite a lot of time. Not every student can move at the same pace, and with a few students arriving late to class, getting everyone involved is more demanding. Liu and Sadler (2000) found that peer response through the MOO feature sometimes put students at a loss as peer responses were usually different, although they came at the same time. The writers often did not know how to react to multiple comments and tended to choose to use simple answers to catch up with communication. In the instruction phrase, it is helpful to use one short text for practice and then reflect on the experience to identify problems among student users. Additionally, the teacher can offer more direct help in using computer software or other features to technically prepare students for such synchronous peer response activities.

## The Timing of Peer Response

The effectiveness of peer response also depends on timing. For instance, a student might receive peer comments between the first and second drafts, or a student might receive peer comments at the same time as the teacher's comments, or a student might receive the teacher's comments prior to peer comments. Ultimately, the timing of peer comments will have an impact on the students' revisions.

Due to the power relations between the teacher and the students in a class, the teacher's comments usually carry more weight than those from peers for the obvious reason that the teacher is the person who determines the grade. Therefore, peer comments received before the teacher's will allow students to revise their drafts independent of the teacher's comments.

It is also important to consider whether we should train our students until they are ready to engage in peer response activities or whether we should consider instruction as part of the peer response activities. That is, should we prepare our students with the knowledge and strategies to respond to their peers' papers before they actually engage in peer response? Or should we wait to instruct our students until they are in the actual process of responding, since we cannot anticipate all the questions that they may have and all the events that may occur? We suggest that instruction be incorporated both prior to peer response via practice sessions (e.g., in small sessions with the instructor) and during the actual process to provide reinforcement and guidance as on-the-spot questions and issues arise.

## Instruction for Revision

As writing teachers, we should also provide concrete revision guidelines based on peer responses and demonstrate how to revise. As Berg (1999, 24) states, "The revision aspect of the instruction is important because it helps writers focus on developing the clarity of their ideas and expressions." Writing teachers can use segments of students' drafts with different foci and synthesize the peer comments received and demonstrate how to revise based on peer response. In doing so, teachers can show students the different aspects of revision needed—such as revisions to content, organization, expression, and grammar—and what should be taken care of first in specific writing samples. For instance, if the draft has both grammatical and content problems, the teacher can demonstrate why changes should be made to the text's content before grammar at the sentence-level is fixed. Another very important purpose of revision instruction is that it can enable students to understand that there is sometimes a discrepancy between intended and perceived meaning. That is to say, students are forced to consider how others have interpreted their writing and whether these interpretations agree with what they meant to convey (Berg 1999).

While it is important to hold students accountable for their peers' comments in order to ensure that they take peer response seriously and make the most of the opportunity to discuss comments with peer responders, it is also important to emphasize that each writer is ultimately responsible for her or his own paper. As such, writers need to be taught to be independent decision makers while still benefiting from peers' comments. In order to achieve this, the following post–peer response activities are suggested.

First of all, after students have had the opportunity to discuss comments with their peers, they should make a list of all the comments/suggestions they received. They then need to carefully decide whether to make the revisions their peers suggested. It may be helpful to provide students with a form that includes five columns (see table 15) so that students can note each comment, who gave it to them, whether or not they will use it in revision, and the reasons for their decision. In other words, students would list each comment, check whether they are going to revise based on this comment, and then, most importantly, justify their decision. This sheet should then be handed in along with the drafts. It can later be

used, for example, in a peer conference with the writer in order to discuss effective revisions. This approach has a number of benefits.

1. It makes it necessary for students to take their peer comments seriously, since they are ultimately responsible
   for deciding whether or not to revise based on these
   comments.
2. It may motivate students to engage in more negotiations
   with their peers during the peer response sessions in order to fully understand the rationale behind their peers'
   suggestions.
3. It helps individual writers become better decision makers about their own writing.

It may be difficult for writers to decide which comments to
utilize for revision and which to ignore. Holding out-of-class
student-teacher conferences at this stage of the writing
process might help the teacher guide students through the de-
cision-making process. These sessions could be held one-on-
one; alternatively, several students could meet with the
teacher at one time, since seeing how others revise their papers based on peer feedback may be helpful to students. As
the students become more familiar with revising based on
peer feedback, short teacher-student consultations can take
place during class time while each student is independently

**TABLE 15.  Revision Feedback Sheet**

| Comment received | Who gave the comment? | Yes—I will revise the paper based on this comment | No—I will not use this comment in revision | Why? |
|---|---|---|---|---|
| 1. | | | | |
| 2. | | | | |
| 3. | | | | |

working on revising in order to ensure that each student is on the right track. Additionally, it is helpful to demonstrate these activities by having students work together with the teacher in revising a draft based on multiple comments. The class could discuss which comments they would utilize and why, and the teacher could then show the students the outcomes of these decisions, or the lack thereof. It is important to continue revision instruction as a whole-class activity throughout the semester so that students constantly get practice in making decisions about what to revise while still receiving the teacher's support and explanations of why something may or may not need to be changed.

Second, after the papers have been revised and submitted for grading, students should get back into their peer response groups in order to have a chance to read their peers' revised papers. This serves a number of purposes: it allows each writer to see the effect of her or his comments on a peer's paper, thus reinforcing the beneficial nature of peer response; it reinforces the nature of the writing process—in other words, the emphasis on multiple drafting—by allowing students to see their peers' writing at different stages; and it reinforces the individual nature of writing—since each writer makes independent decisions about revision—while also suggesting a degree of accountability between the writer and the reviewer(s). The writer needs to be able to justify why he or she did not revise based on a particular comment.

Third, it is valuable to have in-class discussions about the peer response process so that students can reflect on the process, how they benefited from it, what worked and what did not work, and what they would do differently for the next activity. This is important for a number of reasons.

1. Since each class is different, with students at different levels with different needs, a one-type-fits-all approach to peer response does not work. Rather, activities—including questions on peer response forms, the grouping of students, and timing—have to be tailored to each class. That is to say, even if a teacher is teaching two sec-

tions of the same course, the peer response activities and their outcomes will not necessarily be the same across the courses. Nor will they be the same within the same class across different activities. Therefore, it is important that the peer response activities be dynamic—in other words, open to change and flexible to the needs and wants of the learners. Debriefing the learners after activities can help the teacher better understand how the activities can be made more effective.

2. Additionally, having students reflect on the process allows the benefits of peer response to be reinforced, which in turn may motivate students in future peer response activities. This also provides an opportunity to discuss any problems that came up during peer response (e.g., lack of success due to insufficient preparation on the part of students) so that peer response can be more effective next time.

## Suggestions for Teachers

Based on this discussion, we have a number of suggestions for instruction in peer response.

- Instructing our students to successfully complete peer response activities is four-dimensional: affective, cognitive, sociocultural, and linguistic. While each dimension requires specific instructional strategies, they are not mutually exclusive.
- Teachers should be aware of their learners' diverse needs, writing skills, prior peer response experiences, and motivation to engage in peer response before concrete planning can be implemented.
- Teachers should show students what to do and how to do it by using task-specific peer response sheets and concrete examples from previous students' drafts, completed peer response sheets, and revisions based on peers' comments.

- Teachers should provide their own responses on the same task-specific peer response sheets that students use in order to provide a basis of comparison for students. This modeling through the real task teaches students what is desirable and what is not.
- It is beneficial to teach our students how to respond to peers' papers by suggesting some useful expressions.
- Instruction in peer response largely depends on making students aware of intercultural communication competencies based on open-mindedness, politeness, turn-taking strategies, and communicative competence and performance.
- Instruction does not end with the peer response activity. Students also need to be guided in using their peers' comments in revision so that they can become independent decision makers about their own writing.

# Chapter 7
## Making Peer Response Effective

This chapter serves as a synthesis of the salient issues that have been discussed in the preceding chapters, where we look at specific questions or concerns teachers may have in implementing peer response activities. The first section, Problems and Solutions, posits potential issues and concerns teachers may have in classroom practice of peer response and provides concrete ideas to resolve these issues. The Peer Response Checklist is intended for use when teachers prepare in-class peer response activities, to ensure that they have adequately prepared students to respond to and revise their papers.

### Problems and Solutions

**What if students are not prepared with their papers on the date of the peer response activity?**

Unfortunately, this is a common occurrence, and one that many teachers feel is one cause of the failure of peer response in their classes. This situation can be caused by a reluctance to participate in the activities due to anxiety about peers' comments and/or a lack of understanding about the benefits and purpose of the activity. Therefore, although this may occur in the initial stages of peer response, there are a number of things teachers can do to prevent it.

- If students have had instruction in peer response and have understood its purpose and benefits, they may have a greater level of investment in participating in and being prepared for peer response.

- If students have had the opportunity to participate in a practice peer response session—with the instructor and a small group, for example—they may also have a better understanding of the importance of peer response and therefore a greater willingness to participate in peer response activities in class.
- Providing students with sufficient time on a prior class day to prepare their drafts for the peer response activity may also facilitate their readiness.
- Additionally, each group can appoint a person (switching turns across different peer response activities) who is responsible for ensuring that all students are prepared for peer response on a specific day.
- The instructor may also want to have the papers for peer response due the day before the peer response session is to take place in order to ensure that all members have a chance to read the papers carefully before commenting on them. This may also ensure that papers are turned in ahead of time.
- Once groups have been established, students may feel more group pressure to be prepared for peer response—in other words, their group members will expect them to be prepared. This peer pressure in itself may motivate students to be ready for response.
- Along with this, as is discussed in chapter 3, setting up whole-class and individual-group rules for peer response may motivate each student to have a higher level of investment in being prepared for activities. A teacher may want to encourage students to consider issues of preparedness when they establish their own rules to follow in conducting peer response activities. Participating in forming and writing up rules should encourage students to be more invested in following these rules for personal and social reasons.
- Ultimately, the teacher may also want to connect a grade to the students' levels of preparedness for peer response.

While these suggestions may minimize the possibility of a lack of preparation for peer response, they ultimately do not guarantee that students will always be prepared. Therefore, if a student does show up to class without her or his paper for peer response, the teacher has a number of options.

- The student may participate in the peer response activity as a reader only—depending on whether or not the student's class or group has set rules for preparedness, the student may have to participate in peer response outside of class at a later date with one or more of her or his group members.
- The student may orally "read" her or his paper to the group; even though there is no written product, the writer can still get ideas about content and organization from her or his group members.
- The student may still be expected to participate in a peer response activity but to do so out of class, with people that the student finds to read her or his paper. The fact that the student is still held responsible for participating in the peer response activity reemphasizes its importance and will perhaps motivate the student to be better prepared for peer response in the future.

### What if students are absent on peer response day?

This is also a highly likely occurrence, but one that does not need to disrupt the peer response activity. As with lack of preparedness, absence may be one of the issues that students address when they create their own rules for peer response, and therefore, each group may already have guidelines for dealing with this occurrence. We strongly encourage that students still be held responsible for engaging in peer response activities even if they are absent, since this encourages them to take peer response seriously and be well prepared. Thus, if students are absent, they can:

- meet group members (if others are willing!) outside of class time to finish the peer response activity;
- be responsible for finding several outside responders to take the place of the group and have the responders provide the types of comments that are currently being focused on (e.g., content, organization, and/or grammar);
- E-mail or give their paper to a group member who will then be in charge of taking notes and/or tape-recording the peer response comments for the absent student.

### What if students do not get along in their groups?

Even with the best of preparation and instruction in peer response (linguistic, as well as pragmatic and sociocultural), one or more students may not get along. While this may be rare, it can be detrimental to peer response activities. Therefore, we make the following suggestions.

- Teachers should hold initial modeling sessions out of class, with students in small groups, and closely monitor the interactions of students during this instruction. If students do not seem to get along or if the teacher perceives potential problems, they should be regrouped.
- It may be best initially to allow students to self-group, since students tend to work best with those they enjoy being around.
- The teacher should closely monitor peer response activities in class (i.e., sit with each group for a period of time). If issues arise, the teacher can be on hand to help group members negotiate. Thereafter, the teacher can hold a special session with the group and discuss issues such as why problems occurred, how group members felt about them, and how the group thinks it would be best to solve them. This can lead to a revision of rules for peer response for this group or to the creation of new rules; the act of trying to resolve these issues may even create

more group cohesion, since students can address issues they feel are important.

- If a group's problems cannot be resolved, it may be best to regroup its members or split it into dyads.

## What if one or more students dominate the group discussion?

Ideally, because students have discussed turn-taking behavior as part of response instruction and practiced turn-taking in the model peer response session with the teacher, the chances of this occurring will be minimal. It is important that teachers monitor each peer response session by sitting in on each group so that they are aware of the interaction patterns of the members of each group. Additionally, turn-taking behavior should be discussed if and when students create class and/or group rules for peer response. While these actions will all raise student awareness of sharing and participating, they unfortunately will not prevent possible domination by a group member. Should it occur, the following actions may be helpful.

- The teacher may need to remind group members and/or the specific "dominator" of the ground rules for turn-taking—this can be done as an in-class "refreshing" session, which all students may benefit from, or in an individual conference.
- Each group may have a "manager" who monitors the participation of each group member and is assigned to ask a nonparticipant to give their opinions or ask questions and to ask an overly enthusiastic responder to write their comments down and hold off sharing everything until everyone has had a chance to participate. The role of manager can rotate among group members across each peer response task.
- The teacher may create explicit turn-taking guidelines within the group (which may become more lax, as the

students become more familiar with turn-taking, or more strict, if necessary) that require each student in turn to ask one question and/or make one comment and then to hold off making more comments until everyone else has had a turn. This in turn will also facilitate the participation of students who may feel too timid to talk if others dominate.

### What if the computer equipment for the peer response activity does not work?

While technology has done wonders in our lives, it is not completely trouble-free. If computer-mediated peer response is the mode of choice, the teacher will have to invest time in instructing students in using the technology (see chaps. 4 and 6) and ensuring that the computer program runs relatively smoothly. However, what happens before class and what actually takes place during class may be entirely different. Therefore, while the technology appears to work perfectly five minutes before class begins, trouble may still arise during the session. To prevent a virtual shutdown of peer response due to computer technicalities, the teacher is advised to:

- be prepared for problems by having students bring a hard copy (or several copies) of their papers so that the traditional pen-and-paper format can be used if necessary;
- have students exchange disks if they cannot engage in on-line responding;
- have students send attachments or paste their papers into E-mails instead of engaging in on-line responding.

If either of the latter two options is utilized, then students may need to write their comments in bold or italic so that the reader can clearly see what comments have been made and where. Hard copies of the papers can then be printed out so that students can engage in oral peer response based on the written comments; this can help students negotiate the meaning of the comments.

In summary, peer response activities can go smoothly if the teacher plans carefully (including providing pre–, during, and post–peer response guidance for students). If the teacher is enthusiastic about and invested in peer response, then students are likely to be, as well.

The Final Checklist for Peer Response may also help ensure the effectiveness of peer response by providing teachers with a quick way of checking that they have thoroughly prepared students and that no key components have been overlooked.

## Final Checklist for Peer Response

### *Chapter 1*

❏ Students have talked about their experiences with and perceptions of peer response.

❏ The teacher has talked to students about the purpose of peer response, the effects of peer response on revision, and language-skill development in relation to peer response activities.

❏ The teacher has modeled written response behavior in her or his own feedback to students' papers.

### *Chapter 2*

❏ The context in which peer response activities take place has been considered by both the teacher and the students with regard to the feasibility of such activities.

❏ The language of peer response (L1, L2, L1/L2) has been negotiated by the students and teacher. If students' L1 may be used in peer response, the extent of its use has been determined.

❏ Participation modes, norms, and expectations in peer response have been discussed, modeled, and practiced.

❏ The types of tasks and the amount of time allowed for peer response have been modified according to students' age and language proficiency.

❏ Students' skill-area limitations have been taken into consideration in designing peer response activities.

❏ If necessary, vocabulary lists have been made, distributed, and discussed by the writer.

❏ If necessary, writers have clarified the content of their papers before peers read them.

### Chapter 3

❑ Groups have been naturally formed, randomly assigned, or purposefully selected.

❑ Group members have participated in icebreaker activities and/or mini–peer response sessions.

❑ The group leader has been assigned or agreed upon by group members, and the responsibilities of the leader have been determined.

❑ Group rules and goals have been negotiated and agreed upon.

❑ The importance of group cohesion and collaboration has been emphasized.

❑ Reflections on group dynamics, group conflicts, and group concerns have been incorporated into peer response activities.

### Chapter 4

❑ Different modes of peer response have been discussed with the students, and decisions regarding which modes will be used, when, and how have been made.

❑ Students have been reminded to bring written comments on both peer response sheets and peers' critiqued drafts to oral peer response activities.

❑ It has been made clear to students that the purpose of oral peer response is to highlight, discuss, and negotiate, rather than to repeat the major comments made.

❑ Students have practiced using the computer and the software and feel comfortable.

❑ The teacher has checked that the software works on the day of peer response.

❑ Alternative formats for peer response have been planned for (e.g., disk exchange, E-mail, hard copies) in case the software/computer does not work.

❑ Students have been reminded to play active roles in peer response activities, and the consequences of silent participation have been explained.

❑ The author's role during peer response has been established and discussed with the class.

❑ The teacher's various roles (e.g., facilitator, participant, nonparticipant) during peer response have been discussed with the class.

## Chapter 5

❑ The rationale for various foci in peer response has been explained to students.

❑ The task-specific foci of peer response have been negotiated with students.

❑ Appropriate questions and/or peer response sheets have been developed and given and explained to students.

❑ If necessary, minilessons on specific rhetorical, content-based, and grammatical concerns have been conducted prior to peer response.

## Chapter 6

Students have been instructed in:

   ❑  using cognitive strategies;
   ❑  turn-taking behavior;
   ❑  appropriate linguistic expressions;
   ❑  asking revision-oriented questions for clarification.

❑ Students have had the opportunity to practice peer response in groups with the instructor.

❏   The teacher has collected a portfolio of students' sample drafts/peer responses/revisions and used them in practice sessions with students.

❏   Students have been instructed in revising after peer response.

❏   Students have been given sheets to use in listing comments from peers, stating whether they will use these comments for revision, and explaining why or why not.

# References

Allaei, S. K., and U. M. Connor. 1990. Exploring the dynamics of cross-cultural collaboration in writing classrooms. *Writing Instructor* 10:19–28.

Amores, M. J. 1997. A new perspective on peer-editing. *Foreign Language Annals* 30 (4): 513–23.

Beason, L. 1993. Feedback and revision in writing across the curriculum classes. *Research in the Teaching of English* 27:395–421.

Beauvois, M. H., and J. Eledge. 1996. Personality types and megabytes: Student attitudes toward computer mediated communication (CMC) in the language classroom. *CALICO Journal* 13:27–45.

Belcher, D. 1990. Peer vs. teacher response in the advanced composition class. *Issues in Writing* 2 (2): 128–50.

——. Authentic interaction in a virtual classroom: Leveling the playing field in a graduate seminar. *Computers and Composition* 16:253–67.

Belcher, D., and G. Braine. 1995. *Academic writing in a second language: Essays on research and pedagogy.* Norwood, N.J.: Ablex.

Bereiter, C., and M. Scardamalia. 1987. *The psychology of written composition.* Mahwah, N.J.: Lawrence Erlbaum.

Berg, E. C. 1999. The effects of trained peer response on ESL students' revision types and writing quality. *Journal of Second Language Writing* 8 (3): 215–41.

Berger, V. 1990. The effects of peer and self-feedback. *CATESOL Journal* 3:21–35.

Bertcher, H. J. 1979. *Group participations: Techniques for leaders and members.* Thousand Oaks, Calif.: Sage Publications.

Bloch, J., and J. Brutt-Griffler. 2001. Implementing CommonSpace in the ESL composition classroom. In *Linking literacies: Perspectives on L2 reading-writing connections,* ed. D. Belcher and A. Hirvela, 309–34. Ann Arbor: University of Michigan Press.

Braine, G. 1997. Beyond word processing: Networked computers in ESL writing classes. *Computers and Composition* 14:45–58.

Brown, H. D. 2001. *Teaching by principles: An interactive approach to language pedagogy.* White Plains, N.Y.: Pearson Education.

Brown, L. 1991. *Groups for growth and change.* White Plains, N.Y.: Longman.

Bruffee, K. A. 1984. Collaborative learning and the "conversation of mankind." *College English* 46 (7): 635–52.

Caulk, N. 1994. Comparing teacher and student responses to written work. *TESOL Quarterly* 28 (1): 181–88.

Chaudron, C. 1984. The effects of feedback on students' composition revisions. *RELC Journal* 15:1–16.

Cheong, L. K. 1994. Using annotation in a process approach to writing in a Hong Kong classroom. *TESL Reporter* 27 (2): 63–73.

Collier, V. P. 1987. Age and rate of acquisition of second language for academic purposes. *TESOL Quarterly* 21 (4): 617–41.

Connor, U. 1996. *Contrastive Rhetoric.* Cambridge: Cambridge University Press.

Connor, U., and K. Asenavage. 1994. Peer response groups in ESL writing classes: How much impact on revision? *Journal of Second Language Writing* 3 (3): 257–76.

Cummins, J. 1981. The role of primary language development in promoting educational success for language minority students. In *Schooling and language minority students: A theoretical framework,* ed. California State Department of Education, 3–49. Los Angeles: Evaluation, Dissemination, and Assessment Center, California State University.

Deutsch, M. 1962. Cooperation and trust: Some theoretical notes. In *Nebraska Symposium on Motivation,* ed. M. R. Jones, 275–319. Lincoln: University of Nebraska Press.

DiCamilla, F. J., and M. Anton. 1997. Repetition in the collaborative discourse of L2 learners: A Vygotskian perspective. *Canadian Modern Language Review* 53 (4): 609–33.

Donato, R. 1994. Collective scaffolding in second language learning. In *Vygotskian approaches to second language research,* ed. J. P. Lantolf and G. Appel, 33–56. Norwood, N.J.: Ablex.

Doughty, C., and T. Pica. 1986. Information gap tasks: Do they facilitate second language acquisition? *TESOL Quarterly* 20 (2): 305–25.

Dreyer, D. 1992. Responding to peers: The language of native and non-native speakers in writing groups. Ph.D. diss., Indiana University of Pennsylvania. Abstract in *Dissertation Abstracts International* 53 (12): 4237A.

Egbert, J., C. Chao, and E. Hanson-Smith. 1999. Computer-enhanced language learning environments: An overview. In *CALL environments,* ed. J. Egbert and E. Hanson-Smith, 1–16. Alexandria, Va.: TESOL.

Ehrman, M. E., and Z. Dörnyei. 1998. *Interpersonal dynamics in second language education: The visible and invisible classroom.* Thousand Oaks, Calif.: Sage Publications.

Elbow, P. 1973. *Writing without teachers.* New York: Oxford University Press.

Ellis, R. 1994. *The study of second language acquisition.* Oxford: Oxford University Press.

Emig, J. 1971. *The composing processes of twelfth graders.* Research Report No. 13. Urbana, Ill.: National Council of Teachers of English.

Fanderclai, T. L. 1995. MUDs in education: New environment, new pedagogies. *Computer-Mediated Communication Magazine* 2:8–10.

Ferris, D. 1995. Teaching students to self-edit. *TESOL Journal* 4 (4): 18–22.

Ferris, D., and J. Hedgcock. 1998. *Teaching ESL composition: Purpose, process, and practice.* Mahwah, N.J.: Lawrence Erlbaum.

Forsyth, D. R. 1990. *Group dynamics.* 2d ed. Pacific Grove, Calif.: Brooks/Cole.

Gere, A. R. 1987. *Writing groups: History, theory, and implications.* Carbondale: Southern Illinois University Press.

Goffman, E. 1985. *Encounters: Two studies in the sociology of interaction.* New York: Macmillan.

Guerrero, M. C. M. de, and O. S. Villamil. 1994. Socio-cognitive dimensions of interaction in L2 peer revision. *Modern Language Journal* 78 (4): 484–96.

Hansen, J. G. 2001. Teaching process writing through process: A collaborative writing project. Unpublished manuscript.

Hansen, J. G., and J. Liu. 2000. Peer collaboration among community college ESL students. Unpublished manuscript.

Hedgcock, J., and N. Lefkowitz. 1992. Collaborative oral/aural revision in foreign language writing instruction. *Journal of Second Language Writing* 1 (3): 255–76.

Hirvela, A. 1999. Collaborative writing instruction and communities of readers and writers. *TESOL Journal* 8 (2): 7–12.

Hogg, M. A., and D. Abrams. 1988. *Social identifications: A social psychology of intergroup relations and group processes.* New York: Routledge.

Huang, S.-Y. 1996. L1 or L2 peer response sessions? Differences in verbal interactions between a writing group that communicates in Mandarin Chinese and one that uses English. ERIC Document Reproduction Service No. ED400 679.

Huff, R., and C. R. Kline. 1987. *The Contemporary Writing Curriculum: Rehearsing, Composing, and Valuing.* New York: Teachers College Press.

Kamhi-Stein, L. 2000. Adapting U.S.-based TESOL education to meet the needs of nonnative English speakers. *TESOL Journal* 9 (3): 10–14.

Kelm, O. R. 1992. The use of synchronous computer networks in second language instruction: A preliminary report. *Foreign Language Annals* 25 (5): 441–54.

Kern, R. G. 1995. Restructuring classroom interaction with networked computers: Effects on quantity and characteristics of language production. *Modern Language Journal* 79 (4): 457–76.

Kroll, L. R. 1991. Meaning making: Longitudinal aspects of learning to write. Paper presented at the 99th annual meeting of the American Psychological Association, 16–19 August, San Francisco, Calif.

Lantolf, J. P., and G. Appel, eds. 1994. *Vygotskian approaches to second language research.* Norwood, N.J.: Ablex.

Leki, I. 1990. Coaching from the margins: Issues in written response. In *Second language writing: Research insights for the classroom,* ed. B. Kroll, 57–68. New York: Cambridge University Press.

Levine, J. M., and R. L. Moreland. 1990. Progress in small group research. *Annual Review of Psychology* 41:585–634.

Lewin, K. 1948. *Resolving social conflicts: Selected papers on group dynamics.* New York: Harper.

Liu, J. 1996. Perceptions of selected international graduate students towards oral classroom participation in their academic content courses in a United States university. Ph.D. Dissertation, The Ohio State University.

———. 1997. A comparative study of ESL students' pre-/post-conceptualizations of peer review in L2 composition. Paper presented at the 31st annual TESOL Convention, 11–15 March, Orlando, Fla.

———. 1998. Peer review with the instructor: Seeking alternatives in ESL writing. In *Teaching in action: Case studies from second language classrooms,* ed. J. Richards, 237–40. Alexandria, Va.: TESOL.

———. 1999. Nonnative-English-speaking-professionals. *TESOL Quarterly* 33 (1): 85–102.

———. 2000. Understanding Asian Students' Oral Participation Models in American Classrooms. *Journal of Asian Pacific Communication* 10 (1): 155–89.

———. 2001. *Asian students' classroom communication patterns in U.S. universities.* Westport, Conn.: Ablex Publishing.

Liu, J., and R. W. Sadler. 2000. The effects of peer versus teacher comments in both electronic and traditional modes on ESL writers' revisions. Paper presented at the 34th annual TESOL Convention, 14–18 March, Vancouver, British Columbia, Canada.

Lockhart, C., and P. Ng. 1995. Analyzing talk in peer response groups: Stances, functions, and content. *Language Learning* 45:605–55.

Long, M. H. 1985. Input and second language acquisition theory. In *Input in second language acquisition,* ed. S. M. Gass and C. G. Madden, 377–93. Cambridge, Mass.: Newbury House.

Long, M. H., L. Adams, M. McLean, and F. Castaños. 1976. Doing things with words: Verbal interaction in lockstep and small group classroom situations. In *On TESOL '76,* ed. R. Crymes and J. Fanselow, 137–53. Alexandria, Va.: TESOL.

Long, M., and P. Porter. 1985. Group work, interlanguage talk, and second language acquisition. *TESOL Quarterly* 19 (2): 305–25.

MacLennan, B. W., and K. R. Dies. 1992. *Group counseling and psychotherapy with adolescents.* 2d. ed. New York: Columbia University Press.

Mangelsdorf, K. 1989. Parallels between speaking and writing in second language acquisition. In *Richness in writing: Empowering ESL students,* ed. D. M. Johnson and D. H. Roen, 134–45. White Plains, N.Y.: Longman.

———. 1992. Peer reviews in the ESL composition classroom: What do the students think? *ELT Journal* 46 (3): 274–84.

Mangelsdorf, K., and A. Schlumberger. 1992. ESL student response stances in a peer-review task. *Journal of Second Language Writing* 1 (3): 235–54.

McCollom, M. 1990. Group formation: Boundaries, leadership and culture. In *Groups in context: A new perspective on group dynamics,* ed. J. Gilette and M. McCollom, 35–48. Reading, Mass.: Addison-Wesley.

Mendonça, C. O., and K. E. Johnson. 1994. Peer review negotiations: Revision activities in ESL writing instruction. *TESOL Quarterly* 28 (4): 745–69.

Mittan, R. 1989. The peer review process: Harnessing students' communicative power. In *Richness in writing: Empowering ESL students*, ed. D. M. Johnson and D. H. Roen, 207–19. White Plains, N.Y.: Longman.

Moffett, J. 1968. *Teaching the universe of discourse*. Boston: Houghton Mifflin.

Nelson, G. L., and J. G. Carson. 1998. ESL students' perceptions of effectiveness in peer response groups. *Journal of Second Language Writing* 7 (2): 113–31.

Nelson, G. L., and J. M. Murphy. 1992. An L2 writing group: Task and social dimensions. *Journal of Second Language Writing* 1 (3): 171–93.

———. 1993. Peer response groups: Do L2 writers use peer comments in revising their drafts? *TESOL Quarterly* 27 (1): 135–42.

Odlin, T. 1989. *Language transfer*. Cambridge: Cambridge University Press.

Partridge, K. L. 1981. A comparison of the effectiveness of peer vs. teacher evaluation for helping students of English as a second language to improve the quality of their written compositions. Master's thesis, University of Hawaii at Manoa, Honolulu.

Paulus, T. M. 1999. The effect of peer and teacher feedback on student writing. *Journal of Second Language Writing* 8 (3): 265–89.

Peregoy, S. 1989. Relationships between second language oral proficiency and reading comprehension of bilingual fifth grade students. *Journal of the National Association for Bilingual Education* 13 (3): 217–34.

Peregoy, S., and O. Boyle. 1990. Reading and writing scaffolds: Supporting literacy for second language learners. *Educational Issues of Language Minority Students: The Journal* 6:55–67.

———. 2001. *Reading, writing, and learning in ESL: A resource book for K–12 teachers*. White Plains, N.Y.: Longman.

Pica, T., and C. Doughty. 1985. Input and interaction in the communicative language classroom: A comparison of teacher-fronted and group activities. In *Input in second language acquisition*, ed. S. M. Gass and C. G. Madden, 115–32. Rowley, Mass.: Newbury House.

Pica, T., L. Holliday, N. Lewis, and L. Morgenthaler. 1989. Comprehensible output as an outcome of linguistic demands on the learner. *Studies in Second Language Acquisition* 11:63–90.

Porter, P. A. 1983. Variations in the conversations of adult learners of English as a function of the proficiency level of the participants. Ph.D. diss., Stanford University.

———. 1986. How learners talk to each other: Input and interaction in task-centered discussions. In *Talking to learn*, ed. R. R. Day, 200–21. Rowley, Mass.: Newbury House.

Rheingold, H. 1993. A slice of life in my virtual community. In *Global networks: Computers and international communication*, ed. L. M. Harasim, 57–80. Cambridge: MIT Press

Rothschild, D., and F. Klingenberger. 1990. Self and peer evaluation of writing in the interactive ESL classroom: An exploratory study. *TESL Canada Journal* 8:183–204.

Samimy, K., and J. Brutt-Griffler. 1999. Perceptions of NNS students in a graduate TESOL program. In *Nonnative educators in English language teaching,* ed. G. Braine, 129–46. Mahwah, N.J.: Lawrence Erlbaum.

Samway, K. 1987. *The writing processes of non-native English speaking children in elementary grades.* Ph.D. diss., University of Rochester, New York.

Shaw, M. 1981. *Group Dynamics.* 3d ed. New York: McGraw-Hill.

Sproull, L., and S. Kiesler. 1991. *Connections: New ways of working in the networked organization.* Cambridge: MIT Press.

Stanley, J. 1992. Coaching student writers to be effective peer evaluators. *Journal of Second Language Writing* 1 (3): 217–33.

Sullivan, N., and E. Pratt. 1996. A comparative study of two ESL writing environments: A computer-assisted classroom and a traditional oral classroom. *System* 29:491–501.

Swain, M. 1985. Communicative competence: Some roles of comprehensible input and comprehensible output in its development. In *Input in second language acquisition,* ed. S. M. Gass and C. G. Madden, 235–53. Rowley, Mass.: Newbury House.

Tsui, A. 1999. Young ESL writers' responses to peer and teacher comments in writing. In *The Proceedings of the Eighth International Symposium on English Teaching,* ed. Johanna Katchen and Yiu-nam Leung 95–109. Taipei, Taiwan: Crane Publishing.

Urzúa, C. 1987. "You stopped too soon": Second language children composing and revising. *TESOL Quarterly* 21 (2): 279–305.

Varonis, E. M., and S. Gass. 1983. "Target language" input from non-native speakers. Paper presented at the 17th annual TESOL Convention, 15–20 March, Toronto, Ontario, Canada.

Villamil, O. S., and M. C. M. de Guerrero. 1996. Peer revision in the L2 classroom: Social-cognitive activities, mediating strategies, and aspects of social behavior. *Journal of Second Language Writing* 5 (1): 51–75.

———. 1998. Assessing the impact of peer revision on L2 writing. *Applied Linguistics* 19 (4): 491–514.

Vygotsky, L. S. 1978. *Mind in society: The development of higher psychological processes.* Cambridge: Harvard University Press.

Warschauer, M. 1996. Comparing face-to-face and electronic discussion in the second language classroom. *CALICO Journal* 13:7–26.

Watson, H., J. Vallee, and B. Mulford. 1980. *Structured experiences and group development.* Canberra, Australia: Curriculum Development Center.

Wheelan, S. A., and R. L. McKeage. 1993. Development patterns in small and large groups. *Small Group Research* 24:60–83.

Wood, D., J. S. Bruner, and G. Ross. 1976. The role of tutoring in problem solving. *Journal of Child Psychology and Psychiatry* 17:89–100.

Yagelski, R. 1995. The role of classroom context in the revision strategies of student writers. *Research in the Teaching of English* 29:216–38.

Zamel, V. 1982. Writing: The process of discovering meaning. *TESOL Quarterly* 16 (2): 195–209.

——. 1983. The composing process of advanced ESL students: Six case studies. *TESOL Quarterly* 17 (2): 165–87.

——. 1985. Strangers in academia: The experiences of faculty and ESL students across the curriculum. *College Composition and Communication* 46 (4): 506–21.

Zastrow, C. 1989. *Social work with groups.* Chicago: Nelson Hall.

Zhang, S. 1995. Reexamining the affective advantage of peer feedback in the ESL writing class. *Journal of Second Language Writing* 4 (3): 209–22.

Zhu, W. 1995. Effects of training for peer response on students' comments and interaction. *Written Communication* 12:492–528.

# Subject Index

academic literacy skills, 16
active participants, 90–91
adaptability, 139
adult writers, 50
audience awareness, 8
audience expectations, 52

basic intercultural communication
    skills (BICS), 46

classroom participation, 37–39
class size, 32, 40
cognitive strategies, 131
cognitive style, 78
collaborative learning theory, 2–4
collaborative writing, 4
collective scaffolding, 5, 27
communication patterns, 78
communicative competence, 63
comprehensible output, 6
computer-assisted language learning
    (CALL), 80
consciousness-raising activities, 52
content-based instruction, 45, 106
context of peer response, 32
contrastive rhetoric, 111
creativity, 139
cultural backgrounds, 32–34, 38, 39

dual language instruction, 45

effects of peer response, 14, 22–31
    on language development, 27
    long-term, 27, 28
    motivational, 14
    on revision, 22, 25, 84, 85
    short-term, 22–27
E-mail, 21, 43, 76, 83
English as a Foreign Language (EFL),
    44, 45

English for Academic Purposes (EAP),
    53
English Language Development (ELD),
    44, 45
ESL pullout programs, 44, 45

feedback, 1, 16, 17, 23–27, 29, 83, 87,
    124
    peer, 23–27, 29, 83, 87
    self, 23–25
    teacher, 16, 23–27, 29, 83, 87
foci of peer response, 48, 100–121
    combination of features, 117–21
    content, 30, 48, 101, 104–10
        deep content, 107, 108
        surface content, 107
    grammar and style, 30, 36, 37, 48,
        101, 114–17
    rhetoric and organization, 30, 44, 48,
        101, 110–13
foreign language settings, 32, 65

group affiliations, 58
group cohesion, 69, 71, 74
group dynamics, 15, 69
group formation, 60
    by gender and age, 63–64
    heterogeneous groups, 65, 66, 78
    homogeneous groups, 65, 66, 78
    by size, 61–63, 76, 77
    social attraction, 61
    tensions, 66, 67, 71
group goals, 71, 72
grouping, 47, 76
    assigned, 76
    group conflicts, 73, 74
    long-standing, 76
    self-initiated, 76
    task-based, 76
group maintenance, 70
group norms and conformity, 69, 70

group work, 37, 38
group work sustenance, 67
  forming, 67
  mourning/reforming, 67
  norming, 67
  performing, 67
  storming, 67

immersion education, 45
inactive participants, 92, 93
instructing students in peer response,
     25, 27, 29, 122–56
  modes, 140–49
    computer-mediated peer response,
      149–50
    oral peer response, 147–49
    written, 142–49
  rationale, 123–25
  responding, 125–51
  revision, 151–55
intensive English programs (IEPs), 51
interaction and second language
     acquisition, 2, 6, 28

language ability, 19
language development, 27, 28
language use, 34, 35, 101
learners' skill development, 32, 39–41
linguistic background, 32–34, 38, 39
literacy development, 46–48, 51, 52

maintenance bilingual education, 45
modes of peer response, 21, 39, 44, 80,
     81, 88, 101, 102
  asynchronous, 80, 89
  CommonSpace, 86–87, 101
  computer-mediated, 83–89
  computer- mediated communication
    (CMC), 8, 36, 83, 84, 149, 150
  innovative, 81
  MOOs, 83–85
  synchronous, 80, 83, 89
  traditional 81–83

negotiated interaction, 26
negotiation of meaning, 3, 6, 22, 28, 72,
    80, 98

peer editing process, 1, 20
peer response, 1, 7
  perceptions of, 16–19, 20, 21
    cognitive level, 18

communicative level, 18
  textual level, 18
  sheets, 20, 29, 30, 44, 56, 97, 108,
    120, 127, 128, 134–37, 143–48
  tasks, 19
peer response activities, 1, 7, 10
  cognitive benefits, 7
  constraints, 7, 11
  linguistic benefits, 7, 9
  practical, 7, 10
  social benefits, 7, 9
peer review, 1
peer tutoring, 49, 57, 106
perceptions of peer response, 17, 19
  cognitive level, 18
  communicative level, 18
  textual level, 18
portfolio of students' samples, 132
positive classroom atmosphere, 129
process approach, 3, 29, 30, 108
process writing theory, 2, 3, 7
product view, 3
proficiency levels, 54

quality revision, 25, 26
question and comment types in peer
    response, 134–39

revision, 25, 31, 84, 85, 125
  peer, 25
  quality, 25
  self, 25
role in peer response, 20, 42, 56,
    89–97
  author, 94–96
  facilitator, 93, 94, 96
  teacher, 24, 96, 97
  troubleshooter, 96
role reversal, 91, 96

scaffolding, 5, 27, 28, 44, 47, 48
second language acquisition, 2, 6
second language settings, 32, 65, 68
sensitivity, 139
shared linguistic and cultural
    backgrounds, 33
sheltered instruction, 45
social attraction, 61
social identification theory, 61
social interaction, 4, 5, 59
sociocultural competence, 139
somewhat active participants, 91–92

specially designed academic
     instruction in English, 44, 45
surface errors, 100

task achievement, 70
task variation, 15
teacher comments, 21
time-efficiency, 12
timing of peer response, 102, 151

transitional bilingual education, 44, 45
turn-taking, 37, 38, 63, 72
two-way immersion, 45

Vygotsky theory, 4–6, 27

younger writers, 44

Zone of Proximal Development, 4–6

# Author Index

Abrams, D., 61
Adams, L., 6
Allaei, S. K., 7
Amores, M. J., 11, 20
Anton, M., 5, 27
Appel, G., 5
Asenavage, K., 10, 24, 26, 105, 114

Beason, L., 100, 114
Beauvois, M. H., 83
Belcher, D., 23, 53, 83, 84, 105
Bereiter, C., 25
Berg, E. C., 22, 23, 25, 100, 104, 110,
    117, 123, 125, 126, 131, 151, 152
Berger, V., 25, 100, 104, 110, 114, 117
Bertcher, H. J., 58
Bloch, J., 87, 101, 150
Boyle, O., 45, 48, 49, 104, 114
Braine, G., 53, 83
Brown, H. D., 115
Brown, L., 59
Bruffee, K. A., 3, 4
Bruner, J. S., 5
Brutt-Griffler, J., 33, 87, 101, 150

Carson, J. G., 16, 20
Caulk, N., 24–26, 100, 104, 105, 110,
    114, 117
Chao, C., 83
Chaudron, C., 24, 25
Cheong, L. K., 24
Collier, V. P., 46
Connor, U. M., 7, 10, 24, 26, 52, 105,
    114
Cummins, J., 46

Deutsch, M., 61
DiCamilla, F. J., 5, 27
Dies, K. R., 62
Donato, R., 5, 27, 28
Dörnyei, Z., 58, 59

Doughty, C., 6, 10
Dreyer, D., 100, 104, 110, 117

Egbert, J., 83
Ehrman, M. E., 58, 59
Elbow, P., 3
Eledge, J., 83
Ellis, R., 140
Emig, J., 3

Fanderclai, T. L., 83
Ferris, D., 8, 123
Forsyth, D. R., 59, 60

Gass, S., 6
Gere, A. R., 4, 9
Goffman, E., 59
Guerrero, M. C. M. de, 5, 6, 22–28, 101,
    102, 104, 110, 118, 123, 124

Hansen, J. G., 16, 22, 23, 25, 100, 104,
    110, 114, 117, 123, 147
Hanson-Smith, E., 83
Hedgcock, J., 8, 22–26, 100, 104, 105,
    110, 114, 117, 123, 124
Hirvela, A., 4, 9, 124
Hogg, M. A., 61
Holliday, N., 6
Huang, S.-Y., 37, 101, 114
Huff, R., 124

Johnson, K. E., 7–9, 16, 19, 23–25, 28,
    101, 104, 110, 117

Kamhi-Stein, L., 33
Kelm, O. R., 83
Kern, R. G., 83
Kiesler, S., 84
Kline, C. R., 124
Klingenberger, F., 101, 104, 110, 118
Kroll, L. R., 3

Lantolf, J. P., 5
Lefkowitz, N., 22–26, 101, 104, 105, 110, 114, 117, 124
Leki, I., 3, 8–10, 15, 22, 100, 104, 114
Levine, J. M., 64
Lewin, K., 59
Lewis, N., 6
Liu, J., 10, 11, 16, 17, 20, 22, 23, 25, 33, 62, 63, 66, 73, 78, 84, 85, 91, 97, 100, 104, 110, 114, 117, 123, 124, 127, 128, 131, 132, 138, 149, 150
Lockhart, C., 23, 28, 131
Long, M., 6

MacLennan, B. W., 62
Mangelsdorf, K., 3, 10, 15, 24
McCollom, M., 60
McKeage, R. L., 62
McLean, M., 6
Mendonça, C. O., 7–9, 16, 19, 23–25, 28, 101, 104, 110, 117
Mittan, R., 3, 7, 9, 10, 124
Moffett, J., 3
Moreland, R. L., 64
Morgenthaler, L., 6
Mulford, B., 67
Murphy, J. M., 11, 22, 24–26, 104

Nelson, G. L., 11, 16, 20, 22, 24–26, 104
Ng, P., 23, 28, 131

Odlin, T., 46, 52

Partridge, K. L., 24, 28
Paulus, T. M., 22, 24–26, 101, 104, 105, 110, 114, 118
Peregoy, S., 45, 46, 48, 49, 104, 114
Pica, T., 6, 10
Porter, P. A., 6
Pratt, E., 84

Rheingold, H., 83
Ross, G., 5
Rothschild, D., 101, 104, 110, 118

Sadler, R. W., 73, 84, 85, 127, 128, 138, 149, 150
Samimy, K., 33
Samway, K., 48, 104, 110
Scardamalia, M., 25
Schlumberger, A., 3
Shaw, M., 58, 59, 62, 63
Sproull, L., 83
Stanley, J., 22, 23, 25, 124
Sullivan, N., 84
Swain, M., 6

Tsui, A., 24

Urzúa, C., 48, 104, 110

Vallee, J., 67
Varonis, E. M., 6
Villamil, O. S., 5, 6, 22–28, 101, 102, 104, 110, 118, 124
Vygotsky, L. S., 4, 27

Warschauer, M., 84
Watson, H., 67
Wheelan, S. A., 62
Wood, D., 5

Yagelski, R., 100, 104

Zamel, V., 3, 8
Zastrow, C., 59
Zhang, S., 16
Zhu, W., 124